BRITISH BATTLES OF
WORLD WAR I, 1914–15

uncovered editions

Titles in the series

uncovered editions

BRITISH BATTLES OF WORLD WAR I, 1914–15

London: The Stationery Office

First published as Naval and Military Despatches, 1914, 1915, 1916.

© Crown Copyright

This abridged edition
© The Stationery Office 2000
Reprinted with permission.

ISBN 0 11 702447 3

A CIP catalogue record for this book is available from the British Library

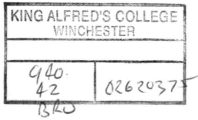
Typeset by J&L Composition, Filey, North Yorkshire
Printed in the United Kingdom for The Stationery Office by Biddles Limited, Guildford, Surrey.

TJ1036   C3   04/00

Uncovered Editions are historic official papers which have not previously been available in a popular form. The series has been created directly from the archive of The Stationery Office in London, and the books have been chosen for the quality of their story-telling. Some subjects are familiar, but others are less well known. Each is a moment of history.

Series editor: Tim Coates

Tim Coates studied at University College, Oxford and at the University of Stirling. After working in the theatre for a number of years, he took up bookselling and became managing director, firstly of Sherratt and Hughes bookshops, and then of Waterstone's. He is known for his support for foreign literature, particularly from the Czech Republic. The idea for "Uncovered Editions" came while searching through the bookshelves of his late father-in-law, Air Commodore Patrick Cave OBE. He is married to Bridget Cave, has two sons, and lives in London.

On 4 August 1914, Britain declared war on Germany. Germany had already invaded Belgium and France and was progressing towards Paris. The events leading up to Britain's declaration of war are described in an earlier volume: War 1914: Punishing the Serbs.

The British Army assembled in London and then travelled by train and ferry to the battle front near Mons. Within days, tens of thousands of young men were to meet their deaths as they joined the ranks of the retreating army.

The despatches in this book were written by the generals at the Front and were published in the "London Gazette", the official newspaper of Parliament. They describe some of the battles that took place in 1914 and 1915, not only in France, but in other places where the British engaged in combat. The accounts here have been transcribed exactly from the material that was written and printed at the time.

The operation to invade the Gallipoli peninsula in 1915 is also covered in the book Lord Kitchener and Winston Churchill: The Dardanelles Part I. *The second part of the Commission's report will be published as* Winston Churchill and the Dardanelles Part II.

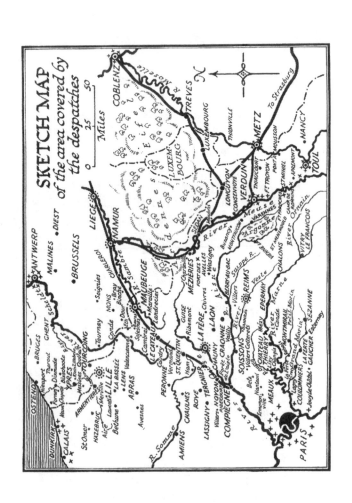

SKETCH MAP
*of the area covered by
the despatches*

Miles
0   25   50

COBLENZ

MOSELLE

TREVES

Eifel

LUXEM-
BOURG

METZ

To Strasburg

NANCY

TOUL

LUXEMBOURG

THIONVILLE

LONGUYON

CONSENVOYE

VERDUN

PONT A MOUSSON

Ardenne

Meuse River

Argonne

VARENNES

ST. MIHIEL

ARGONNY

FT. TROYON

Bazancourt

MONTFAUCON

HEURTEBISE

STENAY

LIÈGE

NAMUR

R. Sambre

CHARLEROI

Charleville

MÉZIÈRES

Chuvres

AVELLES

FORTRESS

WASIGNY

Seraing

Seignies

MONS

Bray

Binche

Dour

Condé

MAUBEUGE

Marville

Marcoing

LE CATEAU

Landrecies

GUISE

Ribemont

LAON

CRAONNE

Forêt de Craonne

R. Aisne

Vesle R.

Aisne River

SOISSONS

Villers

BERRY-AU-BAC

REIMS

Villers Cotterets

Suippe R.

ÉPERNAY

CHÂLONS

Marne R.

VITRY

LE FRANCOIS

SÉZANNE

GAUCHER

ESTERNAY

COULOMMIERS

LA FERTÉ

Petit Morin

CHÂTEAU
THIERRY

R. Condé

MONTMIRAIL

Grand Morin

MEAUX

Fère-en-Tardenois

R. Ourcq

Betz

Emprestlys

Martimont

VILLERS

PARIS

COMPIÈGNE

Fort-en-Tardenois

NOYON

CHAUNY

TERGNIER

LASSIGNY

ROYE

LA FÈRE

ST. QUENTIN

Vermand

Ham

PÉRONNE

CHAULNES

R. Somme

AMIENS

Avesnes

ARRAS

LENS

LA BASSÉE

Béthune

Aire

Lavent

LILLE

HAZEBROUCK

Merville

Armentières

TOURCOING

St. Omer

GHENT

BRUGES

Nieuport

Dixmude

YPRES

POPERINGHE

CALAIS

DUNKIRK

OSTEND

BRUSSELS

MALINES

DIEST

ANTWERP

R. Scheldt

∞◅⋉▷∞

MILITARY DESPATCHES

FROM THE
FIELD-MARSHAL COMMANDING-IN-CHIEF,
BRITISH FORCES IN THE FIELD,
DATED

September 7th and 17th and October 8th, 1914

PUBLISHED IN THE SUPPLEMENTS TO THE
"LONDON GAZETTE", NOS. 28897 AND 28942,
OF SEPTEMBER 9TH AND OCTOBER 19TH, 1914.

War Office, September 9, 1914

The following despatch has been received by the Secretary of State for War from the Field-Marshal Commanding-in-Chief, British Forces in the Field:—

7th September, 1914.

MY LORD,

I have the honour to report the proceedings of the Field Force under my command up to the time of rendering this despatch.

The transport of the troops from England both by sea and by rail was effected in the best order and without a check. Each unit arrived at its destination in this country well within the scheduled time.

The concentration was practically complete on the evening of Friday, the 21st ultimo, and I was able to make dispositions to move the Force during Saturday, the 22nd, to positions I considered most favourable from which to commence operations which the French Commander-in-Chief, General Joffre, requested me to undertake in pursuance of his plans in prosecution of the campaign.

The line taken up extended along the line of the canal from Conde on the west, through Mons and Binche on the east. This line was taken up as follows:—

From Conde to Mons inclusive was assigned to the Second Corps, and to the right of the Second Corps from Mons the First Corps was posted. The 5th Cavalry Brigade was placed at Binche.

In the absence of my Third Army Corps I desired to keep the Cavalry Division as much as possible as a reserve to act on my outer flank, or move in support of any threatened part of the line. The forward reconnaissance was entrusted to Brigadier-General Sir Philip Chetwode with the 5th Cavalry Brigade, but I directed General Allenby to send forward a few squadrons to assist in this work.

During the 22nd and 23rd these advanced squadrons did some excellent work, some of them penetrating as far as Soignies, and several encounters took place in which our troops showed to great advantage.

At 6 a.m., on August 23rd, I assembled the Commanders of the First and Second Corps and Cavalry Division at a point close to the position, and explained the general situation of the Allies, and what I understood to be General Joffre's plan. I discussed with them at some length the immediate situation in front of us.

From information I received from French Headquarters I understood that little more than one, or at most two, of the enemy's Army Corps, with perhaps one Cavalry Division, were in front of my position; and I was aware of no attempted outflanking movement by the enemy. I was confirmed in this opinion by the fact that my patrols encountered no undue opposition in their reconnoitring operations. The observation of my aeroplanes seemed also to bear out this estimate.

About 3 p.m. on Sunday, the 23rd, reports began coming in to the effect that the enemy was commencing an attack on the Mons line, apparently in some strength, but that the right of the position from Mons and Bray was being particularly threatened.

The Commander of the First Corps had pushed his flank back to some high ground south of Bray, and the 5th Cavalry Brigade evacuated Binche, moving slightly south: the enemy thereupon occupied Binche.

The right of the 3rd Division, under General Hamilton, was at Mons, which formed a somewhat dangerous salient; and I directed the Commander of the Second Corps to be careful not to keep the troops on this salient too long, but, if threatened seriously, to draw back the centre behind Mons. This was done before dark. In the meantime, about 5 p.m., I received a most unexpected message from General Joffre by telegraph, telling me that at least three German Corps, viz., a reserve corps, the 4th Corps and the 9th Corps, were moving on my position in front, and that the Second Corps was engaged in a turning movement from the direction of Tournay. He also informed me that the two reserve French Divisions and the 5th French Army on my right were retiring, the Germans having on the previous day gained possession of the passages of the Sambre between Charleroi and Namur.

In view of the possibility of my being driven from the Mons position, I had previously ordered a position in rear to be reconnoitred. This position rested on the fortress of Maubeuge on the right and extended west to Jenlain, south-east of Valenciennes, on the left. The position was reported difficult to hold, because standing crops and buildings made the siting of trenches very difficult and limited the field of fire in many important localities. It nevertheless afforded a few good artillery positions.

When the news of the retirement of the French and the heavy German threatening on my front reached me, I endeavoured to confirm it by aeroplane reconnaissance; and as a result of this I determined to effect a retirement to the Maubeuge position at daybreak on the 24th.

A certain amount of fighting continued along the whole line throughout the night, and at daybreak on the 24th the 2nd Division from the neighbourhood of Harmignies made a powerful demonstration as if to retake Binche. This was supported by the artillery of both the 1st and 2nd Divisions, whilst the 1st Division took up a supporting position in the neighbourhood of Peissant. Under cover of this demonstration the Second Corps retired on the line Dour–Quarouble–Frameries. The 3rd Division on the right of the Corps suffered considerable loss in this operation from the enemy, who had retaken Mons.

The Second Corps halted on this line, where they partially entrenched themselves, enabling Sir Douglas Haig with the First Corps gradually to withdraw to the new position; and he effected this without much further loss, reaching the line Bavai–Maubeuge about

7 p.m. Towards midday the enemy appeared to be directing his principal effort against our left.

I had previously ordered General Allenby with the Cavalry to act vigorously in advance of my left front and endeavour to take the pressure off.

About 7.30 a.m. General Allenby received a message from Sir Charles Fergusson, commanding 5th Division, saying that he was very hard pressed and in urgent need of support. On receipt of this message General Allenby drew in the Cavalry and endeavoured to bring direct support to the 5th Division.

During the course of this operation General De Lisle, of the 2nd Cavalry Brigade, thought he saw a good opportunity to paralyse the further advance of the enemy's infantry by making a mounted attack on his flank. He formed up and advanced for this purpose, but was held up by wire about 500 yards from his objective, and the 9th Lancers and 18th Hussars suffered severely in the retirement of the Brigade.

The 19th Infantry Brigade, which had been guarding the Line of Communications, was brought up by rail to Valenciennes on the 22nd and 23rd. On the morning of the 24th they were moved out to a position south of Quarouble to support the left flank of the Second Corps.

With the assistance of the Cavalry Sir Horace Smith-Dorrien was enabled to effect his retreat to a new position; although, having two corps of the enemy on his front and one threatening his flank, he suffered great losses in doing so.

At nightfall the position was occupied by the

Second Corps to the west of Bavai, the First Corps to the right. The right was protected by the Fortress of Maubeuge, the left by the 19th Brigade in position between Jenlain and Bry, and the Cavalry on the outer flank.

The French were still retiring, and I had no support except such as was afforded by the Fortress of Maubeuge; and the determined attempts of the enemy to get round my left flank assured me that it was his intention to hem me against that place and surround me. I felt that not a moment must be lost in retiring to another position.

I had every reason to believe that the enemy's forces were somewhat exhausted, and I knew that they had suffered heavy losses. I hoped, therefore, that his pursuit would not be too vigorous to prevent me effecting my object.

The operation, however, was full of danger and difficulty, not only owing to the very superior force in my front, but also to the exhaustion of the troops.

The retirement was recommenced in the early morning of the 25th to a position in the neighbourhood of Le Cateau, and rearguards were ordered to be clear of the Maubeuge–Bavai–Eth Road by 5.30 a.m.

Two Cavalry Brigades, with the Divisional Cavalry of the Second Corps, covered the movement of the Second Corps. The remainder of the Cavalry Division with the 19th Brigade, the whole under the command of General Allenby, covered the west flank.

The 4th Division commenced its detrainment at Le Cateau on Sunday, the 23rd, and by the morning of the 25th eleven battalions and a Brigade of Artillery with Divisional Staff were available for service.

I ordered General Snow to move out to take up a position with his right south of Solesmes, his left resting on the Cambrai–Le Cateau Road south of La Chaprie. In this position the Division rendered great help to the effective retirement of the Second and First Corps to the new position.

Although the troops had been ordered to occupy the Cambrai–Le Cateau–Landrecies position, and the ground had, during the 25th, been partially prepared and entrenched, I had grave doubts—owing to the information I received as to the accumulating strength of the enemy against me—as to the wisdom of standing there to fight.

Having regard to the continued retirement of the French on my right, my exposed left flank, the tendency of the enemy's western corps (II.) to envelop me, and, more than all, the exhausted condition of the troops, I determined to make a great effort to continue the retreat till I could put some substantial obstacle, such as the Somme or the Oise, between my troops and the enemy, and afford the former some opportunity of rest and re-organisation. Orders were, therefore, sent to the Corps Commanders to continue their retreat as soon as they possibly could towards the general line Vermand–St. Quentin–Ribemont.

The Cavalry, under General Allenby, were ordered to cover the retirement.

Throughout the 25th and far into the evening, the First Corps continued its march on Landrecies, following the road along the eastern border of the Forêt De Mormal, and arrived at Landrecies about 10 o'clock. I had intended that the Corps should come further west so as to fill up the gap between Le Cateau and Landrecies, but the men were exhausted and could not get further in without rest.

The enemy, however, would not allow them this rest, and about 9.30 p.m. a report was received that the 4th Guards Brigade in Landrecies was heavily attacked by troops of the 9th German Army Corps who were coming through the forest on the north of the town. This brigade fought most gallantly and caused the enemy to suffer tremendous loss in issuing from the forest into the narrow streets of the town. The loss has been estimated from reliable sources at from 700 to 1,000. At the same time information reached me from Sir Douglas Haig that his 1st Division was also heavily engaged south and east of Maroilles. I sent urgent messages to the Commander of the two French Reserve Divisions on my right to come up to the assistance of the First Corps, which they eventually did. Partly owing to this assistance, but mainly to the skilful manner in which Sir Douglas Haig extricated his Corps from an exceptionally difficult position in the darkness of the night, they were able at dawn to resume their march south towards Wessigny on Guise.

By about 6 p.m. the Second Corps had got into position with their right on Le Cateau, their left in the neighbourhood of Caudry, and the line of defence was continued thence by the 4th Division towards Seranvillers, the left being thrown back.

During the fighting on the 24th and 25th the Cavalry became a good deal scattered, but by the early morning of the 26th General Allenby had succeeded in concentrating two brigades to the south of Cambrai.

The 4th Division was placed under the orders of the General Officer Commanding the Second Army Corps.

On the 24th the French Cavalry Corps, consisting of three divisions, under General Sordêt, had been in billets north of Avesnes. On my way back from Bavai, which was my "Poste de Commandement" during the fighting of the 23rd and 24th, I visited General Sordêt, and earnestly requested his co-operation and support. He promised to obtain sanction from his Army Commander to act on my left flank, but said that his horses were too tired to move before the next day. Although he rendered me valuable assistance later on in the course of the retirement, he was unable for the reasons given to afford me any support on the most critical day of all, viz., the 26th.

At daybreak it became apparent that the enemy was throwing the bulk of his strength against the left of the position occupied by the Second Corps and the 4th Division.

At this time the guns of four German Army Corps were in position against them, and Sir Horace

Smith-Dorrien reported to me that he judged it impossible to continue his retirement at daybreak (as ordered) in face of such an attack.

I sent him orders to use his utmost endeavours to break off the action and retire at the earliest possible moment, as it was impossible for me to send him any support, the First Corps being at the moment incapable of movement.

The French Cavalry Corps, under General Sordêt, was coming up on our left rear early in the morning, and I sent an urgent message to him to do his utmost to come up and support the retirement of my left flank; but, owing to the fatigue of his horses he found himself unable to intervene in any way.

There had been no time to entrench the position properly, but the troops showed a magnificent front to the terrible fire which confronted them.

The Artillery, although outmatched by at least four to one, made a splendid fight, and inflicted heavy losses on their opposents.

At length it became apparent that, if complete annihilation was to be avoided, a retirement must be attempted; and the order was given to commence it about 3.30 p.m. The movement was covered with the most devoted intrepidity and determination by the Artillery, which had itself suffered heavily, and the fine work done by the Cavalry in the further retreat from the position assisted materially in the final completion of this most difficult and dangerous operation.

Fortunately the enemy had himself suffered too heavily to engage in an energetic pursuit.

I cannot close the brief account of this glorious stand of the British troops without putting on record my deep appreciation of the valuable services rendered by General Sir Horace Smith-Dorrien.

I say without hesitation that the saving of the left wing of the Army under my command on the morning of the 26th August could never have been accomplished unless a commander of rare and unusual coolness, intrepidity, and determination had been present to personally conduct the operations.

The retreat was continued far into the night of the 26th and through the 27th and 28th, on which date the troops halted on the line Noyon–Chauny–La Fère, having then thrown off the weight of the enemy's pursuit.

On the 27th and 28th I was much indebted to General Sordêt and the French Cavalry Division which he commands for materially assisting my retirement and successfully driving back some of the enemy on Cambrai.

General D'Amade also, with the 61st and 62nd French Reserve Divisions, moved down from the neighbourhood of Arras on the enemy's right flank and took much pressure off the rear of the British Forces.

This closes the period covering the heavy fighting which commenced at Mons on Sunday afternoon, 23rd August, and which really constituted a four days' battle.

At this point, therefore, I propose to close the present despatch.

I deeply deplore the very serious losses which the British Forces have suffered in this great battle; but they were inevitable in view of the fact that the British Army—only two days after a concentration by rail—was called upon to withstand a vigorous attack of five German Army Corps.

It is impossible for me to speak too highly of the skill evinced by the two General Officers command-ing Army Corps; the self-sacrificing and devoted exertions of their Staffs; the direction of the troops by Divisional, Brigade and Regimental Leaders; the command of the smaller units by their officers; and the magnificent fighting spirit displayed by non-commissioned officers and men.

I wish particularly to bring to your Lordship's notice the admirable work done by the Royal Flying Corps under Sir David Henderson. Their skill, energy and perseverance have been beyond all praise. They have furnished me with the most complete and accurate information which has been of incalculable value in the conduct of the operations. Fired at constantly both by friend and foe, and not hesitating to fly in every kind of weather, they have remained undaunted throughout.

Further, by actually fighting in the air, they have succeeded in destroying five of the enemy's machines.

I wish to acknowledge with deep gratitude the incalculable assistance I received from the General and Personal Staffs at Headquarters during this trying period.

Lieutenant-General Sir Archibald Murray, Chief of the General Staff; Major-General Wilson, Sub-Chief of the General Staff; and all under them have worked day and night unceasingly with the utmost skill, self-sacrifice, and devotion; and the same acknowledgment is due by me to Brigadier-General Hon. W. Lambton my Military Secretary, and the Personal Staff.

In such operations as I have described, the work of the Quartermaster-General is of an extremely onerous nature. Major-General Sir William Robertson has met what appeared to be almost insuperable difficulties with his characteristic energy, skill and determination; and it is largely owing to his exertions that the hardships and sufferings of the troops—inseparable from such operations—were not much greater.

Major-General Sir Nevil Macready, the Adjutant-General, has also been confronted with most onerous and difficult tasks in connection with disciplinary arrangements and the preparation of casualty lists. He has been indefatigable in his exertions to meet the difficult situations which arose.

I have not yet been able to complete the list of officers whose names I desire to bring to your Lordship's notice for services rendered during the period under review; and, as I understand it is of importance that this despatch should no longer be delayed, I propose to forward this list, separately, as soon as I can.

I have the honour to be,
Your Lordship's most obedient Servant,
(Signed) J. D. P. FRENCH, Field-Marshal,
Commander-in-Chief,
British Forces in the Field.

∞⧫◊⧫∞

War Office, October 18th, 1914
The following despatches have been received by the
Secretary of State for War from the Field-Marshal
Commanding-in-Chief, British Forces in the
Field:—

17th September, 1914.
My Lord,

In continuation of my despatch of September
7th, I have the honour to report the further progress
of the operations of the Forces under my command
from August 28th.

On that evening the retirement of the Force was

followed closely by two of the enemy's cavalry columns, moving south-east from St. Quentin.

The retreat in this part of the field was being covered by the 3rd and 5th Cavalry Brigades. South of the Somme General Gough, with the 3rd Cavalry Brigade, threw back the Uhlans of the Guard with considerable loss.

General Chetwode, with the 5th Cavalry Brigade, encountered the eastern column near Cérizy, moving south. The Brigade attacked and routed the column, the leading German regiment suffering very severe casualties and being almost broken up.

The 7th French Army Corps was now in course of being railed up from the south to the east of Amiens. On the 29th it nearly completed its detrainment, and the French 6th Army got into position on my left, its right resting on Roye.

The 5th French Army was behind the line of the Oise between La Fère and Guise.

The pursuit of the enemy was very vigorous; some five or six German corps were on the Somme, facing the 5th Army on the Oise. At least two corps were advancing towards my front, and were crossing the Somme east and west of Ham. Three or four more German corps were opposing the 6th French Army on my left.

This was the situation at 1 o'clock on the 29th, when I received a visit from General Joffre at my headquarters.

I strongly represented my position to the French

Commander-in-Chief, who was most kind, cordial, and sympathetic, as he has always been. He told me that he had directed the 5th French Army on the Oise to move forward and attack the Germans on the Somme, with a view to checking pursuit. He also told me of the formation of the Sixth French Army on my left flank, composed of the 7th Army Corps, four Reserve Divisions, and Sordêt's Corps of Cavalry.

I finally arranged with General Joffre to effect a further short retirement towards the line Compiègne–Soissons, promising him, however, to do my utmost to keep always within a day's march of him.

In pursuance of this arrangement the British Forces retired to a position a few miles north of the line Compiègne–Soissons on the 29th.

The right flank of the German Army was now reaching a point which appeared seriously to endanger my line of communications with Havre. I had already evacuated Amiens, into which place a German reserve division was reported to have moved.

Orders were given to change the base to St. Nazaire, and establish an advance base at Le Mans. This operation was well carried out by the Inspector-General of Communications.

In spite of a severe defeat inflicted upon the Guard 10th and Guard Reserve Corps of the German Army by the 1st and 3rd French Corps on the right of the 5th Army, it was not part of General Joffre's plan to pursue this advantage, and a general retirement on to the line of the Marne was ordered, to which the French Forces in the more eastern theatre were directed to conform.

A new Army (the 9th) had been formed from three corps in the south by General Joffre, and moved into the space between the right of the 5th and left of the 4th Armies.

Whilst closely adhering to his strategic conception to draw the enemy on at all points until a favourable situation was created from which to assume the offensive, General Joffre found it necessary to modify from day to day the methods by which he sought to attain this object, owing to the development of the enemy's plans and changes in the general situation.

In conformity with the movements of the French Forces, my retirement continued practically from day to day. Although we were not severely pressed by the enemy, rearguard actions took place continually.

On the 1st September, when retiring from the thickly wooded country to the south of Compiègne, the 1st Cavalry Brigade was overtaken by some German cavalry. They momentarily lost a Horse Artillery battery, and several officers and men were killed and wounded. With the help, however, of some detachments from the 3rd Corps operating on their left, they not only recovered their own guns but succeeded in capturing twelve of the enemy's.

Similarly, to the eastward, the 1st Corps, retiring south, also got into some very difficult forest country, and a somewhat severe rearguard action ensued at Villers-Cotterets, in which the 4th Guards Brigade suffered considerably.

On September 3rd the British Forces were in position south of the Marne between Lagny and Signy-Signets. Up to this time I had been requested by General Joffre to defend the passages of the river as long as possible, and to blow up the bridges in my front. After I had made the necessary dispositions, and the destruction of the bridges had been effected, I was asked by the French Commander-in-Chief to continue my retirement to a point some 12 miles in rear of the position I then occupied, with a view to taking up a second position behind the Seine. This retirement was duly carried out. In the meantime the enemy had thrown bridges and crossed the Marne in considerable force, and was threatening the Allies all along the line of the British Forces and the 5th and 9th French Armies. Consequently several small out-post actions took place.

On Saturday, September 5th, I met the French Commander-in-Chief at his request, and he informed me of his intention to take the offensive forthwith, as he considered conditions were very favourable to success.

General Joffre announced to me his intention of wheeling up the left flank of the 6th Army, pivoting on the Marne and directing it to move on the Ourcq; cross and attack the flank of the 1st German Army, which was then moving in a south-easterly direction east of that river.

He requested me to effect a change of front to my right—my left resting on the Marne and my right on the 5th Army—to fill the gap between that army and the 6th. I was then to advance against the enemy in my front and join in the general offensive movement.

These combined movements practically commenced on Sunday, September 6th, at sunrise; and on that day it may be said that a great battle opened on a front extending from Ermenonville, which was just in front of the left flank of the 6th French Army, through Lizy on the Marne, Mauperthuis, which was about the British centre, Courtecon, which was the left of the 5th French Army, to Esternay and Charleville, the left of the 9th Army under General Foch, and so along the front of the 9th, 4th, and 3rd French Armies to a point north of the fortress of Verdun.

This battle, in so far as the 6th French Army, the British Army, the 5th French Army and the 9th French Army were concerned, may be said to have concluded on the evening of September 10th, by which time the Germans had been driven back to the line Soissons–Reims, with a loss of thousands of prisoners, many guns, and enormous masses of transport.

About the 3rd September the enemy appears to have changed his plans and to have determined to stop his advance South direct upon Paris; for on the 4th September air reconnaissances showed that his main columns were moving in a south-easterly direction generally east of a line drawn through Nanteuil and Lizy on the Ourcq.

On the 5th September several of these columns were observed to have crossed the Marne; whilst

German troops, which were observed moving south-east up the left bank of the Ourcq on the 4th, were now reported to be halted and facing that river. Heads of the enemy's columns were seen crossing at Changis, La Ferté, Nogent, Château Thierry and Mezy.

Considerable German columns of all arms were seen to be converging on Montmirail, whilst before sunset large bivouacs of the enemy were located in the neighbourhood of Coulommiers, south of Rebais, La Ferté-Gaucher and Dagny.

I should conceive it to have been about noon on the 6th September, after the British Forces had changed their front to the right and occupied the line Jouy–Le Chatel–Faremoutiers–Villeneuve Le Comte, and the advance of the 6th French Army north of the Marne towards the Ourcq became apparent, that the enemy realised the powerful threat that was being made against the flank of his columns moving south-east, and began the great retreat which opened the battle above referred to.

On the evening of the 6th September, therefore, the fronts and positions of the opposing armies were roughly as follows:—

ALLIES

6th French Army.—Right on the Marne at Meux, left towards Betz.

British Forces.—On the line Dagny–Coulommiers–Maison.

5th French Army.—At Courtagon, right on Esternay.

Conneau's Cavalry Corps.—Between the right of the British and the left of the French 5th Army.

GERMANS

4th Reserve and 2nd Corps.—East of the Ourcq and facing that river.

9th Cavalry Division.—West of Crecy.

2nd Cavalry Division.—North of Coulommiers.

4th Corps.—Rebais.

3rd and 7th Corps.—South-West of Montmirail.

All these troops constituted the 1st German Army, which was directed against the French 6th Army on the Ourcq, and the British Forces, and the left of the 5th French Army south of the Marne.

The 2nd German Army (IX., X., X.R. and Guard) was moving against the centre and right of the 5th French Army and the 9th French Army.

On the 7th September both the 5th and 6th French Armies were heavily engaged on our flank. The 2nd and 4th Reserve German Corps on the Ourcq vigorously opposed the advance of the French towards that river, but did not prevent the 6th Army from gaining some headway, the Germans themselves suffering serious losses. The French 5th Army threw the enemy back to the line of the Petit Morin river after inflicting severe losses upon them, especially about Montceaux, which was carried at the point of the bayonet.

The enemy retreated before our advance, covered by his 2nd and 9th and Guard Cavalry Divisions, which suffered severely.

Our Cavalry acted with great vigour, especially General De Lisle's Brigade with the 9th Lancers and 18th Hussars.

On the 8th September the enemy continued his retreat northward, and our Army was successfully engaged during the day with strong reargards of all arms on the Petit Morin River, thereby materially assisting the progress of the French Armies on our right and left, against whom the enemy was making his greatest efforts. On both sides the enemy was thrown back with very heavy loss. The First Army Corps encountered stubborn resistance at La Trétoire (north of Rebais). The enemy occupied a strong position with infantry and guns on the northern bank of the Petit Morin River; they were dislodged with considerable loss. Several machine guns and many prisoners were captured, and upwards of two hundred German dead were left on the ground.

The forcing of the Petit Morin at this point was much assisted by the Cavalry and the 1st Division, which crossed higher up the stream.

Later in the day a counter attack by the enemy was well repulsed by the First Army Corps, a great many prisoners and some guns again falling into our hands.

On this day (8th September) the Second Army Corps encountered considerable opposition, but drove back the enemy at all points with great loss, making considerable captures.

The Third Army Corps also drove back considerable bodies of the enemy's infantry and made some captures.

On the 9th September the First and Second Army Corps forced the passage of the Marne and advanced some miles to the north of it. The Third Corps encountered considerable opposition, as the bridge at La Ferté was destroyed and the enemy held the town on the opposite bank in some strength, and thence persistently obstructed the construction of a bridge; so the passage was not effected until after nightfall.

During the day's pursuit the enemy suffered heavy loss in killed and wounded, some hundreds of prisoners fell into our hands and a battery of eight machine guns was captured by the 2nd Division.

On this day the 6th French Army was heavily engaged west of the River Ourcq. The enemy had largely increased his force opposing them; and very heavy fighting ensued, in which the French were successful throughout.

The left of the 5th French Army reached the neighbourhood of Château Thierry after the most severe fighting, having driven the enemy completely north of the river with great loss.

The fighting of this Army in the neighbourhood of Montmirail was very severe.

The advance was resumed at daybreak on the 10th up to the line of the Ourcq, opposed by strong rearguards of all arms. The 1st and 2nd Corps, assisted by the Cavalry Division on the right, the 3rd and 5th Cavalry Brigades on the left, drove the enemy northwards. Thirteen guns, seven machine guns, about 2,000 prisoners, and quantities of transport fell into our hands. The enemy left many dead on the field. On this day the French 5th and 6th Armies had little opposition.

As the 1st and 2nd German Armies were now in full retreat, this evening marks the end of the battle which practically commenced on the morning of the 6th instant; and it is at this point in the operations that I am concluding the present despatch.

Although I deeply regret to have had to report heavy losses in killed and wounded throughout these operations, I do not think they have been excessive in view of the magnitude of the great fight, the outlines of which I have only been able very briefly to describe, and the demoralisation and loss in killed and wounded which are known to have been caused to the enemy by the vigour and severity of the pursuit.

In concluding this despatch I must call your Lordship's special attention to the fact that from Sunday, August 23rd, up to the present date (September 17th), from Mons back almost to the Seine, and from the Seine to the Aisne, the Army under my command has been ceaselessly engaged without one single day's halt or rest of any kind.

Since the date to which in this despatch I have limited my report of the operations, a great battle on the Aisne has been proceeding. A full report of this battle will be made in an early further despatch.

It will, however, be of interest to say here that, in spite of a very determined resistance on the part of the enemy, who is holding in strength and great tenacity a position peculiarly favourable to defence, the battle which commenced on the evening of the 12th instant has, so far, forced the enemy back from his first position, secured the passage of the river, and inflicted great loss upon him, including the capture of over 2,000 prisoners and several guns.

I have the honour to be,
Your Lordship's most obedient Servant,
(Signed) J. D. P. FRENCH, Field-Marshal,
Commanding-in-Chief,
The British Forces in the Field.

8th October, 1914.

My Lord,

I have the honour to report the operations in which the British Forces in France have been engaged since the evening of the 10th September.

In the early morning of the 11th the further pursuit of the enemy was commenced; and the three Corps crossed the Ourcq practically unopposed, the Cavalry reaching the line of the Aisne River; the 3rd and 5th Brigades south of Soissons, the 1st, 2nd and 4th on the high ground at Couvrelles and Cerseuil.

On the afternoon of the 12th from the opposition encountered by the 6th French Army to the west of Soissons, by the 3rd Corps south-east of that place, by the 2nd Corps south of Missy and Vailly, and certain indications all along the line, I formed the opinion that the enemy had, for the moment at any rate, arrested his retreat and was preparing to dispute the passage of the Aisne with some vigour.

South of Soissons the Germans were holding Mont de Paris against the attack of the right of the French 6th Army when the 3rd Corps reached the neighbourhood of Buzancy, south-east of that place. With the assistance of the Artillery of the 3rd Corps the French drove them back across the river at Soissons, where they destroyed the bridges.

The heavy artillery fire which was visible for several miles in a westerly direction in the valley of the Aisne showed that the 6th French Army was meeting with strong opposition all along the line.

On this day the Cavalry under General Allenby reached the neighbourhood of Braine and did good work in clearing the town and the high ground beyond it of strong hostile detachments. The Queen's Bays are particularly mentioned by the General as having assisted greatly in the success of this operation. They were well supported by the 3rd Division, which on this night bivouacked at Brenelle, south of the river.

The 5th Division approached Missy, but were unable to make headway.

The 1st Army Corps reached the neighbourhood of Vauxcéré without much opposition.

In this manner the Battle of the Aisne commenced.

The Aisne Valley runs generally East and West, and
consists of a flat-bottomed depression of width varying from half a mile to two miles, down which the
river follows a winding course to the West at some
points near the southern slopes of the valley and at
others near the northern. The high ground both on
the north and south of the river is approximately 400
feet above the bottom of the valley and is very similar in character, as are both slopes of the valley itself,
which are broken into numerous rounded spurs and
re-entrants. The most prominent of the former are
the Chivre spur on the right bank and Sermoise spur
on the left. Near the latter place the general plateau
on the south is divided by a subsidiary valley of much
the same character, down which the small River Vesle
flows to the main stream near Sermoise. The slopes of
the plateau overlooking the Aisne on the north and
south are of varying steepness, and are covered with
numerous patches of wood, which also stretch
upwards and backwards over the edge on to the top
of the high ground. There are several villages and
small towns dotted about in the valley itself and along
its sides, the chief of which is the town of Soissons.

The Aisne is a sluggish stream of some 170 feet in
breadth, but, being 15 feet deep in the centre, it is
unfordable. Between Soissons on the west and Villers
on the east (the part of the river attacked and secured
by the British Forces) there are eleven road bridges

across it. On the north bank a narrow-gauge railway runs from Soissons to Vailly, where it crosses the river and continues eastward along the south bank. From Soissons to Sermoise a double line of railway runs along the south bank, turning at the latter place up the Vesle Valley towards Bazoches.

The position held by the enemy is a very strong one, either for a delaying action or for a defensive battle. One of its chief military characteristics is that from the high ground on neither side can the top of the plateau on the other side be seen except for small stretches. This is chiefly due to the woods on the edges of the slopes. Another important point is that all the bridges are under either direct or high-angle artillery fire.

The tract of country above described, which lies north of the Aisne, is well adapted to concealment, and was so skilfully turned to account by the enemy as to render it impossible to judge the real nature of his opposition to our passage of the river, or to accurately gauge his strength; but I have every reason to conclude that strong rearguards of at least three army corps were holding the passages on the early morning of the 13th.

On that morning I ordered the British Forces to advance and make good the Aisne.

The 1st Corps and the Cavalry advanced on the river. The 1st Division was directed on Chanouille via the canal bridge at Bourg, and the 2nd Division on Courtecon and Presles via Pont-Arcy and on the canal to the north of Braye via Chavonne. On the right the Cavalry and 1st Division met with slight opposition, and found a passage by means of the canal which crosses the river by an aqueduct. The Division was therefore able to press on, supported by the Cavalry Division on its outer flank, driving back the enemy in front of it.

On the left the leading troops of the 2nd Division reached the river by 9 o'clock. The 5th Infantry Brigade were only enabled to cross, in single file and under considerable shell fire, by means of the broken girder of the bridge which was not entirely submerged in the river. The construction of a pontoon bridge was at once undertaken, and was completed by 5 o'clock in the afternoon.

On the extreme left the 4th Guards Brigade met with severe opposition at Chavonne, and it was only late in the afternoon that it was able to establish a foothold on the northern bank of the river by ferrying one battalion across in boats.

By nightfall the 1st Division occupied the area Moulins–Paissy–Geny, with posts in the village of Vendresse.

The 2nd Division bivouacked as a whole on the southern bank of the river, leaving only the 5th Brigade on the north bank to establish a bridge head.

The Second Corps found all the bridges in front of them destroyed, except that of Condé, which was in possession of the enemy, and remained so until the end of the battle.

In the approach to Missy, where the 5th Division eventually crossed, there is some open ground which was swept by heavy fire from the opposite bank. The

13th Brigade was, therefore, unable to advance; but the 14th, which was directed to the east of Venizel at a less exposed point, was rafted across, and by night established itself with its left at St. Marguérite. They were followed by the 15th Brigade; and later on both the 14th and 15th supported the 4th Division on their left in repelling a heavy counter-attack on the Third Corps.

On the morning of the 13th the Third Corps found the enemy had established himself in strength on the Vregny Plateau. The road bridge at Venizel was repaired during the morning, and a reconnaissance was made with a view to throwing pontoon bridge at Soissons.

The 12th Infantry Brigade crossed at Venizel, and was assembled at Bucy Le Long by 1 p.m., but the bridge was so far damaged that artillery could only be man-handled across it. Meanwhile the construction of a bridge was commenced close to the road bridge at Venizel.

At 2 p.m. the 12th Infantry Brigade attacked in the direction of Chivres and Vregny with the object of securing the high ground east of Chivres, as a necessary preliminary to a further advance northwards. This attack made good progress, but at 5.30 p.m. the enemy's artillery and machine-gun fire from the direction of Vregny became so severe that no further advance could be made. The positions reached were held till dark.

The pontoon bridge at Venizel was completed at 5.30 p.m., when the 10th Infantry Brigade crossed the river and moved to Bucy Le Long.

The 19th Infantry Brigade moved to Billy Sur Aisne, and before dark all the artillery of the Division had crossed the river, with the exception of the Heavy Battery and one Brigade of Field Artillery.

During the night the positions gained by the 12th Infantry Brigade to the east of the stream running through Chivres were handed over to the 5th Division.

The section of the Bridging Train allotted to the Third Corps began to arrive in the neighbourhood of Soissons late in the afternoon, when an attempt to throw a heavy pontoon bridge at Soissons had to be abandoned, owing to the fire of the enemy's heavy howitzers.

In the evening the enemy retired at all points and entrenched himself on the high ground about two miles north of the river along which runs the Chemin-des-Dames. Detachments of Infantry, however, strongly entrenched in commanding points down slopes of the various spurs, were left in front of all three corps with powerful artillery in support of them.

During the night of the 13th and on the 14th and following days the Field Companies were incessantly at work night and day. Eight pontoon bridges and one footbridge were thrown across the river under generally very heavy artillery fire, which was incessantly kept up on to most of the crossings after completion. Three of the road bridges, *i.e.*, Venizel, Missy and Vailly, and the railway bridge east of Vailly were temporarily repaired so as to take foot traffic and the

Villers Bridge made fit to carry weights up to six tons.

Preparations were also made for the repair of the Missy, Vailly and Bourg Bridges so as to take mechanical transport.

The weather was very wet and added to the difficulties by cutting up the already indifferent approaches, entailing a large amount of work to repair and improve.

The operations of the Field Companies during this most trying time are worthy of the best traditions of the Royal Engineers.

On the evening of the 14th it was still impossible to decide whether the enemy was only making a temporary halt, covered by rearguards, or whether he intended to stand and defend the position.

With a view to clearing up the situation, I ordered a general advance.

The action of the First Corps on this day under the direction and command of Sir Douglas Haig was of so skilful, bold and decisive a character that he gained positions which alone have enabled me to maintain my position for more than three weeks of very severe fighting on the north bank of the river.

The Corps was directed to cross the line Moulins–Moussy by 7 a.m.

On the right the General Officer Commanding the 1st Division directed the 2nd Infantry Brigade (which was in billets and bivouacked about Moulins), and the 25th Artillery Brigade (less one battery),

under General Bulfin, to move forward before daybreak, in order to protect the advance of the Division
sent up the valley to Vendresse. An officers' patrol sent
out by this Brigade reported a considerable force of
the enemy near the factory north of Troyon, and the
Brigadier accordingly directed two regiments (the
King's Royal Rifles and the Royal Sussex Regiment)
to move at 3 a.m. The Northamptonshire Regiment
was ordered to move at 4 a.m. to occupy the spur east
of Troyon. The remaining regiment of the Brigade
(the Loyal North Lancashire Regiment) moved at
5.30 a.m. to the village of Vendresse. The factory was
found to be held in considerable strength by the
enemy, and the Brigadier ordered the Loyal North
Lancashire Regiment to support the King's Royal
Rifles and the Sussex Regiment. Even with this support the force was unable to make headway, and on
the arrival of the 1st Brigade the Coldstream Guards
were moved up to support the right of the leading
Brigade (the 2nd), while the remainder of the 1st
Brigade supported its left.

About noon the situation was, roughly, that the
whole of these two brigades were extended along a
line running east and west, north of the line Troyon
and south of the Chemin-des-Dames. A party of the
Loyal North Lancashire Regiment had seized and
were holding the factory. The enemy held a line of
entrenchments north and east of the factory in considerable strength, and every effort to advance against
this line was driven back by heavy shell and machine-
gun fire. The morning was wet and a heavy mist hung

over the hills, so that the 25th Artillery Brigade and the Divisional Artillery were unable to render effective support to the advanced troops until about 9 o'clock.

By 10 o'clock the 3rd Infantry Brigade had reached a point one mile south of Vendresse, and from there it was ordered to continue the line of the 1st Brigade and to connect with and help the right of the 2nd Division. A strong hostile column was found to be advancing, and by a vigorous counter stroke with two of his battalions the Brigadier checked the advance of this column and relieved the pressure on the 2nd Division. From this period until late in the afternoon the fighting consisted of a series of attacks and counter attacks. The counter strokes by the enemy were delivered at first with great vigour, but later on they decreased in strength, and all were driven off with heavy loss.

On the left the 6th Infantry Brigade had been ordered to cross the river and to pass through the line held during the preceding night by the 5th Infantry Brigade and occupy the Courtecon Ridge, whilst a detached force, consisting of the 4th Guards Brigade and the 36th Brigade, Royal Field Artillery, under Brigadier-General Perceval, were ordered to proceed to a point east of the village of Ostel.

The 6th Infantry Brigade crossed the river at Pont-Arcy, moved up the valley towards Braye, and at 9 a.m. had reached the line Tilleul–La Buvelle. On this line they came under heavy artillery and rifle fire, and were unable to advance until supported by the

34th Brigade, Royal Field Artillery, and the 44th Howitzer Brigade and the Heavy Artillery.

The 4th Guards Brigade crossed the river at 10 a.m. and met with very heavy opposition. It had to pass through dense woods; field artillery support was difficult to obtain; but one section of a field battery pushed up to and within the firing line. At 1 p.m. the left of the Brigade was south of the Ostel Ridge.

At this period of the action the enemy obtained a footing between the First and Second Corps, and threatened to cut the communications of the latter.

Sir Douglas Haig was very hardly pressed and had no reserve in hand. I placed the Cavalry Division at his disposal, part of which he skilfully used to prolong and secure the left flank of the Guards Brigade. Some heavy fighting ensued, which resulted in the enemy being driven back with heavy loss.

About 4 o'clock the weakening of the counter attacks by the enemy and other indications tended to show that his resistance was decreasing, and a general advance was ordered by the Army Corps Commander. Although meeting with considerable opposition and coming under very heavy artillery and rifle fire, the position of the corps at the end of the day's operations extended from the Chemin-des-Dames on the right, through Chivy, to Le Cour de Soupir, with the 1st Cavalry Brigade extending to the Chavonne–Soissons road.

On the right the corps was in close touch with the French Moroccan troops of the 18th Corps, which were entrenched in échelon to its right rear. During the night they entrenched this position.

Throughout the Battle of the Aisne this advanced and commanding position was maintained, and I cannot speak too highly of the valuable services rendered by Sir Douglas Haig and the Army Corps under his command. Day after day and night after night the enemy's infantry has been hurled against him in violent counter attack which has never on any one occasion succeeded, whilst the trenches all over his position have been under continuous heavy artillery fire.

The operations of the First Corps on this day resulted in the capture of several hundred prisoners, some field pieces, and machine guns.

The casualties were very severe, one brigade alone losing three of its four Colonels.

The 3rd Division commenced a further advance and had nearly reached the plateau of Aizy when they were driven back by a powerful counter attack supported by heavy artillery. The division, however, fell back in the best order, and finally entrenched itself about a mile north of Vailly Bridge, effectively covering the passage.

The 4th and 5th Divisions were unable to do more than maintain their ground.

On the morning of the 15th, after close examination of the position, it became clear to me that the enemy was making a determined stand; and this view was confirmed by reports which reached me from the French Armies fighting on my right and left, which clearly showed that a strongly entrenched line of defence was being taken up from the north of Compiègne, eastward and south-eastward, along the whole valley of the Aisne up to and beyond Reims.

A few days previously the Fortress of Maubeuge fell, and a considerable quantity of siege artillery was brought down from that place to strengthen the enemy's position in front of us.

During the 15th shells fell in our position which have been judged by experts to be thrown by eight-inch siege guns with a range of 10,000 yards. Throughout the whole course of the battle our troops have suffered very heavily from this fire, although its effect latterly was largely mitigated by more efficient and thorough entrenching, the necessity for which I impressed strongly upon Army Corps Commanders. In order to assist them in this work all villages within the area of our occupation were searched for heavy entrenching tools, a large number of which were collected.

In view of the peculiar formation of the ground on the north side of the river between Missy and Soissons, and its extraordinary adaptability to a force on the defensive, the 5th Division found it impossible to maintain its position on the southern edge of the Chivres Plateau, as the enemy in possession of the village of Vregny to the west was able to bring a flank fire to bear upon it. The Division had, therefore, to retire to a line the left of which was the village of Marguérite, and thence ran by the north edge of Missy back to the river to the east of that place.

With great skill and tenacity Sir Charles Fergusson maintained this position throughout the whole battle, although his trenches were necessarily on lower ground than that occupied by the enemy on the southern edge of the plateau, which was only 400 yards away.

General Hamilton with the 3rd Division vigorously attacked to the north, and regained all the ground he had lost on the 15th, which throughout the battle has formed a most powerful and effective bridge head.

On the 16th the 6th Division came up into line.

It had been my intention to direct the First Corps to attack and seize the enemy's position on the Chemin-des-Dames, supporting it with this new reinforcement. I hoped from the position thus gained to bring effective fire to bear across the front of the 3rd Division, which, by securing the advance of the latter, would also take the pressure off the 5th Division and the Third Corps.

But any further advance of the First Corps would have dangerously exposed my right flank. And, further, I learned from the French Commander-in-Chief that he was strongly reinforcing the 6th French Army on my left, with the intention of bringing up the Allied left to attack the enemy's flank and thus compel his retirement. I therefore sent the 6th Division to join the Third Corps with orders to keep it on the south side of the river, as it might be available in general reserve.

On the 17th, 18th and 19th the whole of our line was heavily bombarded, and the First Corps was constantly and heavily engaged. On the afternoon of the 17th the right flank of the 1st Division was seriously threatened. A counter attack was made by the Northamptonshire Regiment in combination with the Queen's, and one battalion of the Divisional Reserve was moved up in support. The Northamptonshire Regiment, under cover of mist, crept up to within a hundred yards of the enemy's trenches and charged with the bayonet, driving them out of the trenches and up the hill. A very strong force of hostile infantry was then disclosed on the crest line. This new line was enfiladed by part of the Queen's and the King's Royal Rifles, which wheeled to their left on the extreme right of our infantry line, and were supported by a squadron of cavalry on their outer flank. The enemy's attack was ultimately driven back with heavy loss.

On the 18th, during the night, the Gloucestershire Regiment advanced from their position near Chivy, filled in the enemy's trenches and captured two maxim guns.

On the extreme right the Queen's were heavily attacked, but the enemy was repulsed with great loss. About midnight the attack was renewed on the First Division, supported by artillery fire, but was again repulsed.

Shortly after midnight an attack was made on the left of the 2nd Division with considerable force, which was also thrown back.

At about 1 p.m. on the 19th the 2nd Division drove back a heavy infantry attack strongly supported by artillery fire. At dusk the attack was renewed and again repulsed.

On the 18th I discussed with the General Officer Commanding the Second Army Corps and his Divisional Commanders the possibility of driving the enemy out of Condé, which lay between his two Divisions, and seizing the bridge which has remained throughout in his possession.

As, however, I found that the bridge was closely commanded from all points on the south side and that satisfactory arrangements were made to prevent any issue from it by the enemy by day or night, I decided that it was not necessary to incur the losses which an attack would entail, as, in view of the position of the Second and Third Corps, the enemy could make no use of Condé, and would be automatically forced out of it by any advance which might become possible for us.

On this day information reached me from General Joffre that he had found it necessary to make a new plan, and to attack and envelop the German right flank.

It was now evident to me that the battle in which we had been engaged since the 12th instant must last some days longer until the effect of this new flank movement could be felt and a way opened to drive the enemy from his positions.

It thus became essential to establish some system of regular relief in the trenches, and I have used the infantry of the 6th Division for this purpose with good results. The relieved brigades were brought back alternately south of the river, and, with the artillery of the 6th Division, formed a general reserve on which I could rely in case of necessity.

The Cavalry has rendered most efficient and ready help in the trenches, and have done all they possibly could to lighten the arduous and trying task which has of necessity fallen to the lot of the Infantry.

On the evening of the 19th and throughout the 20th the enemy again commenced to show considerable activity. On the former night a severe counter-attack on the 3rd Division was repulsed with considerable loss, and from early on Sunday morning various hostile attempts were made on the trenches of the 1st Division. During the day the enemy suffered another severe repulse in front of the 2nd Division, losing heavily in the attempt. In the course of the afternoon the enemy made desperate attempts against the trenches all along the front of the First Corps, but with similar results.

After dark the enemy again attacked the 2nd Division, only to be again driven back.

Our losses on these two days were considerable, but the number, as obtained, of the enemy's killed and wounded vastly exceeded them.

As the troops of the First Army Corps were much exhausted by this continual fighting, I reinforced Sir Douglas Haig with a brigade from the reserve, and called upon the 1st Cavalry Division to assist them.

On the night of the 21st another violent counter-attack was repulsed by the 3rd Division, the enemy losing heavily.

On the 23rd the four six-inch howitzer batteries, which I had asked to be sent from home, arrived. Two batteries were handed over to the Second Corps and two to the First Corps. They were brought into action on the 24th with very good results.

Our experiences in this campaign seem to point to the employment of more heavy guns of a larger calibre in great battles which last for several days, during which time powerful entrenching work on both sides can be carried out.

These batteries were used with considerable effect on the 24th and the following days.

On the 23rd the action of General de Castelnau's Army on the Allied left developed considerably, and apparently withdrew considerable forces of the enemy away from the centre and east. I am not aware whether it was due to this cause or not, but until the 26th it appeared as though the enemy's opposition in our front was weakening. On that day, however, a very marked renewal of activity commenced. A constant and vigorous artillery bombardment was maintained all day, and the Germans in front of the 1st Division were observed to be "sapping" up to our lines and trying to establish new trenches. Renewed counter-attacks were delivered and beaten off during the course of the day, and in the afternoon a well-timed attack by the 1st Division stopped the enemy's entrenching work.

During the night of 27th–28th the enemy again made the most determined attempts to capture the trenches of the 1st Division, but without the slightest success.

Similar attacks were reported during these three days all along the line of the Allied front, and it is certain that the enemy then made one last great effort to establish ascendency. He was, however, unsuccessful everywhere, and is reported to have suffered heavy losses. The same futile attempts were made all along our front up to the evening of the 28th, when they died away, and have not since been renewed.

On former occasions I have brought to your Lordship's notice the valuable services performed during this campaign by the Royal Artillery.

Throughout the Battle of the Aisne they have displayed the same skill, endurance and tenacity, and I deeply appreciate the work they have done.

Sir David Henderson and the Royal Flying Corps under his command have again proved their incalculable value. Great strides have been made in the development of the use of aircraft in the tactical sphere by establishing effective communication between aircraft and units in action.

It is difficult to describe adequately and accurately the great strain to which officers and men were subjected almost every hour of the day and night throughout this battle.

I have described above the severe character of the artillery fire which was directed from morning till night, not only upon the trenches, but over the whole surface of the ground occupied by our Forces. It was not until a few days before the position was evacuated that the heavy guns were removed and the fire slackened. Attack and counter-attack occurred at all hours of the night and day throughout the whole position, demanding extreme vigilance, and permitting only a minimum of rest.

The fact that between the 12th September to the date of this despatch the total numbers of killed, wounded and missing reached the figures amounting to 561 officers, 12,980 men, proves the severity of the struggle.

The tax on the endurance of the troops was further increased by the heavy rain and cold which prevailed for some ten or twelve days of this trying time.

The Battle of the Aisne has once more demonstrated the splendid spirit, gallantry and devotion which animates the officers and men of His Majesty's Forces.

With reference to the last paragraph of my despatch of September 7th, I append the names of officers, non-commissioned officers and men brought forward for special mention by Army Corps commanders and heads of departments for services rendered from the commencement of the campaign up to the present date.

I entirely agree with these recommendations and beg to submit them for your Lordship's consideration.

I further wish to bring forward the names of the following officers who have rendered valuable service:—General Sir Horace Smith-Dorrien and Lieutenant-General Sir Douglas Haig (commanding First and Second Corps respectively) I have already mentioned in the present and former despatches for particularly marked and distinguished service in critical situations.

Since the commencement of the compaign they have carried out all my orders and instructions with the utmost ability.

Lieutenant-General W. P. Pulteney took over the command of the Third Corps just before the commencement of the Battle of the Marne. Throughout the subsequent operations he showed himself to be a most capable commander in the field and has rendered very valuable services.

Major-General E. H. H. Allenby and Major-General H. de la P. Gough have proved themselves to be Cavalry leaders of a high order, and I am deeply indebted to them. The undoubted moral superiority which our Cavalry has obtained over that of the enemy has been due to the skill with which they have turned to the best account the qualities inherent in the splendid troops they command.

In my despatch of 7th September I mentioned the name of Brigadier-General Sir David Henderson and his valuable work in command of the Royal Flying Corps; and I have once more to express my deep appreciation of the help he has since rendered me.

Lieutenant-General Sir Archibald Murray has continued to render me invaluable help as Chief of the Staff; and in his arduous and responsible duties he has been ably assisted by Major-General Henry Wilson, Sub-Chief.

Lieutenant-General Sir Nevil Macready and Lieutenant-General Sir William Robertson have continued to perform excellent service as Adjutant-General and Quartermaster-General respectively.

The Director of Army Signals, Lieutenant-Colonel J. S. Fowler, has materially assisted the operations by the skill and energy which he has displayed in the working of the important department over which he presides.

My Military Secretary, Brigadier-General the Hon. W. Lambton, has performed his arduous and difficult duties with much zeal and great efficiency.

I am anxious also to bring to your Lordship's notice the following names of officers of my Personal Staff, who throughout these arduous operations have shown untiring zeal and energy in the performance of their duties:—

Aides-de-Camp.
Lieutenant-Colonel Stanley Barry.
Lieutenant-Colonel Lord Brooke.
Major Fitzgerald Watt.

Extra Aide-de-Camp.
Captain the Hon. F. E. Guest.

Private Secretary.
Lieutenant-Colonel Brindsley Fitzgerald.

Major His Royal Highness Prince Arthur of Connaught, K.G., joined my Staff as Aide-de-Camp on the 14th September.

His Royal Highness's intimate knowledge of languages enabled me to employ him with great advantage on confidential missions of some importance, and his services have proved of considerable value.

I cannot close this despatch without informing your Lordship of the valuable services rendered by the Chief of the French Military Mission at my Headquarters, Colonel Victor Huguet, of the French Artillery. He has displayed tact and judgment of a high order in many difficult situations, and has rendered conspicuous service to the Allied cause.

I have the honour to be,
Your Lordship's most obedient Servant,
(Signed) J. D. P. FRENCH, Field-Marshal,
Commanding-in-Chief,
The British Army in the Field.

∞∞❧❧∞∞

MILITARY DESPATCH

DATED
5th December 1914

The following despatch has been received from Field-Marshal Sir J. D. P. French, G.C.B., G.C.V.O., K.C.M.G., covering a despatch from Major-General A. Paris, C.B., R.M.A., relating to the operations round Antwerp from the 3rd to the 9th October.

From Sir J. D. P. French, Field-Marshal, Commanding-in-Chief, to the Secretary of the Admiralty.

In forwarding this report to the Army Council at the request of the Lords Commissioners of the Admiralty, I have to state that, from a comprehensive review of all the circumstances, the force of Marines and Naval Brigades which assisted in the defence of Antwerp was handled by General Paris with great skill and boldness.

Although the results did not include the actual saving of the fortress, the action of the force under General Paris certainly delayed the enemy for a considerable time, and assisted the Belgian Army to be withdrawn in a condition to enable it to reorganize and refit, and regain its value as a fighting force. The destruction of war material and ammunition—which, but for the intervention of this force, would have proved of great value to the enemy—was thus able to be carried out.

The assistance which the Belgian Army has rendered throughout the subsequent course of the operations on the canal and the Yeser river has been a valuable asset to the allied cause, and such help must be regarded as an outcome of the intervention of General Paris's force. I am further of opinion that the moral effect produced on the minds of the Belgian Army by this necessarily desperate attempt to bring them succour, before it was too late, has been of great value to their use and efficiency as a fighting force.

J. D. P. FRENCH,
Field-Marshal,
Commanding-in-Chief.

From the Secretary of the Admiralty to Field-Marshal Sir J. D. P. French, Commanding-in-Chief.

Admiralty, 2nd November, 1914.

SIR,

I AM commanded by My Lords Commissioners of the Admiralty to transmit herewith a despatch from Major-General Paris, reporting the proceeding of the Division round Antwerp from the 3rd to 9th October, with a view to its being considered by you and forwarded to the Army Council with your survey of the operations as a whole.

I am, etc.,

W. GRAHAM GREENE.

From Major-General A. Paris, C.B., Commanding Royal Naval Division, to the Secretary of the Admiralty.

31st October, 1914.

Regarding the operations round Antwerp from 3rd to 9th October, I have the honour to report as follows:—

The Brigade (2,200 all ranks) reached Antwerp during the night 3rd–4th October, and early on the 4th occupied, with the 7th Belgian Regiment, the trenches facing Lierre, with advanced post on the River Nethe, relieving some exhausted Belgian troops.

The outer forts on this front had already fallen and bombardment of the trenches was in progress. This increased in violence during the night and early morning of 5th October, when the advanced posts were driven in and the enemy effected a crossing of the river, which was not under fire from the trenches.

About midday the 7th Belgian Regiment was forced to retire, thus exposing my right flank. A vigorous counter-attack, gallantly led by Colonel Tierchon, 2nd Chasseurs, assisted by our aeroplanes, restored the position late in the afternoon.

Unfortunately, an attempt made by the Belgian troops during the night (5th–6th October) to drive the enemy across the river failed, and resulted in the evacuation of practically the whole of the Belgian trenches.

The few troops now capable of another counter-attack were unable to make any impression, and the position of the Marine Brigade became untenable.

The bombardment, too, was very violent, but the retirement of the Brigade was well carried out, and soon after midday (6th October) an intermediate position, which had been hastily prepared, was occupied.

The two Naval Brigades reached Antwerp during the night, 5th–6th October. The 1st Brigade moved out in the afternoon of 5th to assist the withdrawal to the main 2nd Line of Defence.

The retirement was carried out during the night, 6th–7th October, without opposition, and the Naval Division occupied the intervals between the forts on the 2nd Line of Defence.

The bombardment of the town, forts and trenches began at midnight, 7th–8th October, and continued with increasing intensity until the evacuation of the fortress.

As the water supply had been cut, no attempt could be made to subdue the flames, and soon 100 houses were burning. Fortunately, there was no wind, or the whole town and bridges must have been destroyed.

During the day (8th October) it appeared evident that the Belgian Army could not hold the forts any longer. About 5.30 p.m. I considered that if the Naval Division was to avoid disaster an immediate retirement under cover of darkness was necessary. General De Guise, the Belgian Commander, was in complete agreement. He was most chivalrous and gallant, insisting on giving orders that the roads and bridges were to be cleared for the passage of the British troops.

The retirement began about 7.30 p.m., and was carried out under very difficult conditions.

The enemy were reported in force (a Division plus a Reserve Brigade) on our immediate line of retreat, rendering necessary a detour of 15 miles to the north.

All the roads were crowded with Belgian troops, refugees, herds of cattle, and all kinds of vehicles, making inter-communication a practical impossibility. Partly for these reasons, partly on account of fatigue, and partly from at present unexplained causes large numbers of the 1st Naval Brigade became detached, and I regret to say are either prisoners or interned in Holland.

Marching all night (8th to 9th October), one battalion of 1st Brigade, the 2nd Brigade and Royal Marine Brigade, less one battalion, entrained at St. Gillies Waes and effected their retreat without further incident.

The Battalion (Royal Marine Brigade) Rear Guard of the whole force, also entrained late in the afternoon together with many hundreds of refugees, but at Morbeke the line was cut, the engine derailed, and the enemy opened fire.

There was considerable confusion. It was dark and the agitation of the refugees made it difficult to pass any orders. However, the battalion behaved admirably, and succeeded in fighting its way through, but with a loss in missing of more than half its number. They then marched another 10 miles to Selzaate and entrained there.

Colonel Seely and Colonel Bridges were not part of my command, but they rendered most skilful and helpful services during the evacuation.

The casualties are approximately—

1st Naval Brigade and 2nd Naval Brigade, 5 killed, 64 wounded, 2,040 missing.

Royal Marine Brigade, 23 killed, 103 wounded, 388 missing.

∞⚬≫◇≪⚬∞

CAPTURE OF THE GERMAN CRUISER "EMDEN" BY H.M.A.S. "SYDNEY" on Monday 9th November, 1914

PUBLISHED IN THE SUPPLEMENTS TO THE "LONDON GAZETTE", NO. 29025 OF 1ST JANUARY, 1915.

Admiralty, 1st January, 1915.

The following despatch has been received from Captain John C. T. Glossop, reporting the capture of the German Cruiser "Emden" by H.M.A.S. "Sydney".

The Cocos Islands (Keeling Islands)

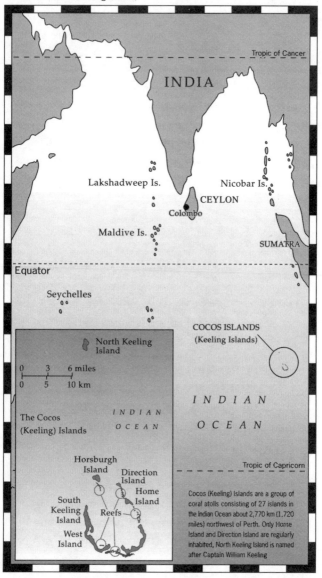

Tropic of Cancer

INDIA

Lakshadweep Is.

Nicobar Is.

CEYLON

Colombo

Maldive Is.

SUMATRA

Equator

Seychelles

North Keeling
Island

0   3   6 miles
0   5   10 km

The Cocos
(Keeling) Islands

INDIAN

OCEAN

COCOS ISLANDS
(Keeling Islands)

INDIAN

OCEAN

Tropic of Capricorn

Horsburgh
Island

Direction
Island

Home
Island

South
Keeling
Island

Reefs

West
Island

Cocos (Keeling) Islands are a group of
coral atolls consisting of 27 islands in
the Indian Ocean about 2,770 km (1,720
miles) northwest of Perth. Only Home
Island and Direction Island are regularly
inhabited. North Keeling Island is named
after Captain William Keeling

H.M.A.S. "Sydney" at Colombo,
15th November, 1914.

Sir,

I HAVE the honour to report that whilst on escort duty with the Convoy under the charge of Captain Silver, H.M.A.S. "Melbourne," at 6.30 a.m., on Monday, 9th November, a wireless message from Cocos was heard reporting that a foreign warship was off the entrance. I was ordered to raise steam for full speed at 7.0 a.m. and proceed thither. I worked up to 20 knots, and at 9.15 a.m. sighted land ahead and almost immediately the smoke of a ship, which proved to be H.I.G.M.S. "Emden" coming out towards me at a great rate. At 9.40 a.m. fire was opened, she firing the first shot. I kept my distance as much as possible to obtain the advantage of my guns. Her fire was very accurate and rapid to begin with, but seemed to slacken very quickly, all casualties occurring in this ship almost immediately. First the foremost funnel of her went, secondly the foremast, and she was badly on fire aft, then the second funnel went, and lastly the third funnel, and I saw she was making for the beach on North Keeling Island, where she grounded at 11.20 a.m. I gave her two more broadsides and left her to pursue a merchant ship which had come up during the action.

Although I had guns on this merchant ship at odd times during the action I had not fired, and as she was making off fast I pursued and overtook her at 12.10, firing a gun across her bows, and hoisting International Code Signal to stop, which she did. I sent an armed boat and found her to be the S.S. "Buresk," a captured British collier, with 18 Chinese crew, 1 English Steward, 1 Norwegian Cook, and a German Prize Crew of 3 Officers, 1 Warrant Officer and 12 men. The ship unfortunately was sinking, the Kingston knocked out and damaged to prevent repairing, so I took all on board, fired 4 shells into her and returned to "Emden," passing men swimming in the water, for whom I left 2 boats I was towing from "Buresk."

On arriving again off "Emden" she still had her colours up at mainmast head. I enquired by signal, International Code, "Will you surrender?" and received a reply in Morse "What signal? No signal books." I then made in Morse "Do you surrender?" and subsequently "Have you received my signal?" to neither of which did I get an answer. The German Officers on board gave me to understand that the Captain would never surrender, and therefore, though reluctantly, I again fired at her at 4.30 p.m., ceasing at 4.35, as she showed white flags and hauled down her ensign by sending a man aloft.

I then left "Emden" and returned and picked up the "Buresk's" two boats, rescuing 2 sailors (5.0 p.m.), who had been in the water all day. I returned and sent in one boat to "Emden," manned by her own prize crew from "Buresk," and 1 Officer, and stating I would return to their assistance next morning. This I had to do, as I was desirous to find out the condition of cables and Wireless Station at Direction Island. On the passage over I was again delayed by rescuing another sailor (6.30 p.m.), and by the time I was again ready and approaching Direction Island it was too late for the night.

I lay on and off all night and communicated with Direction Island at 8.0 a.m., 10th November, to find that the "Emden's" party consisting of 3 officers and 40 men, 1 launch and 2 cutters had seized and provisioned a 70 tons schooner (the "Ayesha"), having 4 Maxims, with 2 belts to each. They left the previous night at six o'clock. The Wireless Station was entirely destroyed, 1 cable cut, 1 damaged, and 1 intact. I borrowed a Doctor and 2 Assistants, and proceeded as fast as possible to "Emden's" assistance.

I sent an Officer on board to see the Captain, and in view of the large number of prisoners and wounded and lack of accommodation, &c., in this ship, and the absolute impossibility of leaving them where they were, he agreed that if I received his Officers and men and all wounded, "then as for such time as they remained in 'Sydney' they would cause no interference with ship or fittings, and would be amenable to the ship's discipline." I therefore set to work at once to tranship them—a most difficult operation, the ship being on weather side of Island and the send alongside very heavy. The conditions in the "Emden" were indescribable. I received the last from her at 5.0 p.m., then had to go round to the lee side to pick up 20 more men who had managed to get ashore from the ship.

Darkness came on before this could be accomplished, and the ship again stood off and on all night, resuming operations at 5.0 a.m. on 11th November, a cutter's crew having to land with stretchers to bring wounded round to embarking point. A German Officer, a Doctor, died ashore the previous day. The ship in the meantime ran over to Direction Island to return their Doctor and Assistants, send cables, and was back again at 10.0 a.m., embarked the remainder of wounded, and proceeded for Colombo by 10.35 a.m. Wednesday, 11th November.

Total casualties in "Sydney": Killed 3, severely wounded (since dead) 1, severely wounded 4, wounded 4, slightly wounded 4. In the "Emden" I can only approximately state the killed at 7 Officers and 108 men from Captain's statement. I had on board 11 Officers, 9 Warrant Officers, and 191 men, of whom 3 Officers and 53 men were wounded, and of this number 1 Officer and 3 men have since died of wounds.

The damage to "Sydney's" hull and fittings was surprisingly small; in all about 10 hits seem to have been made. The engine and boiler rooms and funnels escaped entirely.

I have great pleasure in stating that the behaviour of the ship's company was excellent in every way, and with such a large proportion of young hands and people under training it is all the more gratifying. The engines worked magnificently, and higher results than trials were obtained, and I cannot speak too highly of the Medical Staff and arrangements on subsequent trip, the ship being nothing but a hospital of a most painful description.

∞⦿∞

PROCEEDINGS OF THE FLOTILLA OFF THE COAST OF BELGIUM
between the 17th October and 9th November, 1914.

PUBLISHED IN THE SUPPLEMENTS TO THE "LONDON GAZETTE", NO. 29126 OF 13TH APRIL, 1915.

Admiralty, 13th April, 1915.

The following despatch has been received from Rear-Admiral the Hon. Horace L. A. Hood, C.B., M.V.O., D.S.O., reporting the proceedings of the flotilla off the coast of Belgium between 17th October and 9th November, 1914:—

Office of Rear-Admiral, Dover Patrol,
11th November, 1914.

Sir,

I have the honour to report the proceedings of the flotilla acting off the coast of Belgium, between October 17th and November 9th.

The flotilla was organised to prevent the movement of large bodies of German troops along the coast roads from Ostend to Nieuport, to support the left flank of the Belgian Army, and to prevent any movement by sea of the enemy's troops.

Operations commenced during the night of October 17th, when the "Attentive," flying my flag, accompanied by the monitors "Severn," "Humber," and "Mersey," the light cruiser "Foresight," and several torpedo-boat destroyers, arrived and anchored off Nieuport Pier.

Early on the morning of the 18th October information was received that German infantry were advancing on Westende village, and that a battery was in action at Westende Bains. The flotilla at once proceeded up past Westende and Middlekirke to draw the fire and endeavour to silence the guns.

A brisk shrapnel fire was opened from the shore, which was immediately replied to, and this commenced the naval operations on the coast which continued for more than three weeks without intermission.

During the first week the enemy's troops were endeavouring to push forward along the coast roads, and a large accumulation of transport existed within reach of the naval guns.

On October 18th machine guns from the "Severn" were landed at Nieuport to assist in the defence, and Lieutenant E. S. Wise fell, gallantly leading his men.

The "Amazon," flying my flag, was badly holed on the waterline and was sent to England for repairs, and during these early days most of the vessels suffered casualties, chiefly from shrapnel shell from the field guns of the enemy.

The presence of the ships on the coast soon caused alterations in the enemy's plans, less and less of their troops were seen, while more and more heavy guns were gradually mounted among the sand dunes that fringe the coast.

It soon became evident that more and heavier guns were required in the flotilla. The Scouts therefore returned to England, while H.M.S. "Venerable" and several older cruisers, sloops and gunboats arrived to carry on the operations.

Five French torpedo-boat destroyers were placed under my orders by Admiral Favereau, and on the 30th October I had the honour of hoisting my flag in the "Intrépide" and leading the French flotilla into action off Lombartzyde. The greatest harmony and enthusiasm existed between the allied flotillas.

As the heavier guns of the enemy came into play it was inevitable that the casualties of the flotilla increased, the most important being the disablement of the 6-inch turret and several shots on the waterline of the "Mersey," the death of the Commanding Officer and eight men and the disablement of 16 others in the "Falcon," which vessel came under a heavy fire when guarding the "Venerable" against submarine attack; the "Wildfire" and "Vestal" were badly holed, and a number of casualties caused in the "Brilliant" and "Rinaldo."

Enemy submarines were seen and torpedoes were fired, and during the latter part of the operations the work of the torpedo craft was chiefly confined to the protection of the larger ships.

It gradually became apparent that the rush of the enemy along the coast had been checked, that the operations were developing into a trench warfare, and that the work of the flotilla had, for the moment, ceased.

MEMORANDUM BY THE DIRECTOR OF
THE AIR DEPARTMENT

PUBLISHED IN THE SUPPLEMENT TO THE "LONDON
GAZETTE", NO. 29025, OF 1ST JANUARY, 1915.

Admiralty, 17th December, 1914.

On 21st November, 1914, Squadron Commander E.
F. Briggs, Flight Commander J. T. Babington, and
Flight Lieutenant S. V. Sippe, Royal Navy, carried out
an aerial attack on the Zeppelin airship sheds and
factory at Friedrickshafen on Lake Constance.

Aerial attack, Friedrickshafen November 1914

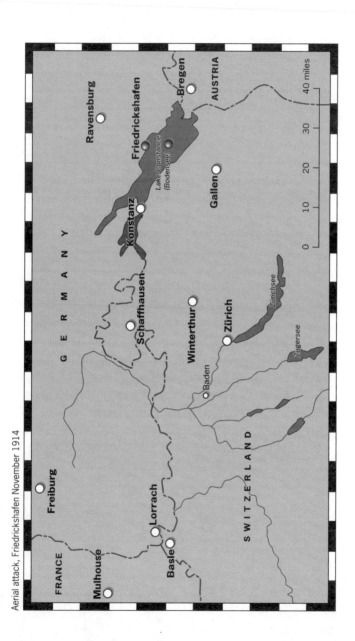

Leaving French Territory shortly before 10 a.m., they arrived over their objective at about noon, and, although under a very heavy rifle, machine-gun and shrapnel fire from the moment they were sighted, they all three dived steeply to within a few hundred feet of the sheds, when they released their bombs—in all eleven.

Squadron Commander Briggs was wounded, brought down, and made a prisoner, but the other two officers regained their starting-point after a flight of more than four hours across hostile country under very bad weather conditions.

It is believed that the damage caused by this attack includes the destruction of one airship and serious damage to the larger shed, and also demolition of the hydrogen-producing plant, which had only lately been completed. Later reports stated that flames of considerable magnitude were seen issuing from the factory immediately after the raid.

∞⚬❌⚬∞

MILITARY DESPATCHES
FROM THE
FIELD-MARSHAL COMMANDING-IN-CHIEF,
BRITISH FORCES IN THE FIELD
DATED
2nd February, 1915

PUBLISHED IN THE SUPPLEMENT TO THE "LONDON GAZETTE", NO. 29069, OF 16TH FEBRUARY, 1915.

The following Despatch was received on the 12th February, 1915:—

General Headquarters, 2nd February, 1915.

MY LORD,

I have the honour to forward a further report on the operations of the Army under my command.

In the period under review the salient feature was the presence of His Majesty the King in the Field. His Majesty arrived at Headquarters on the 30th November, and left on the 5th December.

At a time when the strength and endurance of the troops had been tried to the utmost throughout the long and arduous Battle of Ypres-Armentières the presence of His Majesty in their midst was of the greatest possible help and encouragement.

His Majesty visited all parts of the extensive area of operations and held numerous inspections of the troops behind the line of trenches.

On the 16th November Lieutenant His Royal Highness the Prince of Wales, K.G., Grenadier Guards, joined my Staff as Aide-de-Camp.

Since the date of my last report the operations of the Army under my command have been subject almost entirely to the limitations of weather.

History teaches us that the course of campaigns in Europe, which have been actively prosecuted during the months of December and January have been largely influenced by weather conditions. It should, however, be thoroughly understood throughout the country that the most recent development of armaments and the latest methods of conducting warfare have added greatly to the difficulties and drawbacks of a vigorous winter campaign.

To cause anything more than a waste of ammunition long-range artillery fire requires constant and accurate observation; but this most necessary condition is rendered impossible of attainment in the midst of continual fog and mist.

Again, armies have now grown accustomed to rely largely on aircraft reconnaissance for accurate information of the enemy; but the effective performance of this service is materially influenced by wind and weather.

The deadly accuracy, range and quick-firing capabilities of the modern rifle and machine gun require that a fire-swept zone be crossed in the shortest possible space of time by attacking troops. But if men are detained under the enemy's fire by the difficulty of emerging from a water-logged trench, and by the necessity of passing over ground knee-deep in holding mud and slush, such attacks become practically prohibitive owing to the losses they entail.

During the exigencies of the heavy fighting which ended in the last week of November the French and British Forces had become somewhat mixed up, entailing a certain amount of difficulty in matters of supply and in securing unity of command.

By the end of November I was able to concentrate the Army under my command in one area, and, by holding a shorter line, to establish effective reserves.

By the beginning of December there was a considerable falling off in the volume of artillery fire directed against our front by the enemy. Reconnaissance and reports showed that a certain amount of artillery had been withdrawn. We judged that the cavalry in our front, with the exception of one Division of the Guard, had disappeared.

There did not, however, appear to have been any great diminution in the numbers of infantry holding the trenches.

Although both artillery and rifle fire were exchanged with the enemy every day, and sniping went on more or less continuously during the hours of daylight, the operations which call for special record or comment are comparatively few.

During the last week in November some successful minor night operations were carried out in the 4th Corps.

On the night of the 23rd–24th November a small party of the 2nd Lincolnshire Regiment, under Lieutenant E. H. Impey, cleared three of the enemy's advanced trenches opposite the 25th Brigade and withdrew without loss.

On the night of the 24th–25th Captain J. R. Minshull Ford, Royal Welsh Fusiliers, and Lieutenant E. L. Morris, Royal Engineers, with 15 men of the Royal Engineers and Royal Welsh Fusiliers, successfully mined and blew up a group of farms immediately in front of the German trenches on the Touquet Bridoux Road which had been used by German snipers.

On the night of the 26th–27th November a small party of the 2nd Scots Guards, under Lieutenant Sir E. H. W. Hulse, Bt., rushed the trenches opposite the 20th Brigade; and after pouring a heavy fire into them returned with useful information as to the strength of the Germans and the position of machine guns.

The trenches opposite the 25th Brigade were rushed the same night by a patrol of the 2nd Rifle Brigade, under Lieutenant E. Durham.

On the 23rd November the 112th Regiment of the 14th German Army Corps succeeded in capturing some 800 yards of the trenches held by the Indian Corps, but the General Officer Commanding the Meerut Division organized a powerful counter-attack, which lasted throughout the night. At daybreak on the 24th November the line was entirely re-established.

The operation was a costly one, involving many casualties, but the enemy suffered far more heavily.

We captured over 100 prisoners, including 3 officers, as well as 3 machine guns and 2 trench mortars.

On December 7th the concentration of the Indian Corps was completed by the arrival of the Sirhind Brigade from Egypt.

On December 9th the enemy attempted to commence a strong attack against the 3rd Corps, particularly in front of the trenches held by the Argyll and Sutherland Highlanders and the Middlesex Regiment.

They were driven back with heavy loss, and did not renew the attempt. Our casualties were very slight.

During the early days of December certain indications along the whole front of the Allied Line induced the French Commanders and myself to believe that the enemy had withdrawn considerable forces from the Western Theatre.

Arrangements were made with the Commander of the 8th French Army for an attack to be commenced on the morning of December 14th.

Operations began at 7 a.m. by a combined heavy artillery bombardment by the two French and the 2nd British Corps.

The British objectives were the Petit Bois and the Maedelsteed Spur, lying respectively to the west and south-west of the village of Wytschaete.

At 7.45 a.m. the Royal Scots, with great dash, rushed forward and attacked the former, while the Gordon Highlanders attacked the latter place.

The Royal Scots, commanded by Major F. J. Duncan, D.S.O., in face of a terrible machine-gun and rifle fire, carried the German trench on the west edge of the Petit Bois, capturing two machine-guns and 53 prisoners, including one officer.

The Gordon Highlanders, with great gallantry, advanced up the Maedelsteed Spur, forcing the enemy to evacuate their front trench. They were, however, losing heavily, and found themselves unable to get any further. At nightfall they were obliged to fall back to their original position.

Captain C. Boddam-Whetham and Lieutenant W. F. R. Dobie showed splendid dash, and with a few men entered the enemy's leading trenches; but they were all either killed or captured.

Lieutenant G. R. V. Hume-Gore and Lieutenant W. H. Paterson also distinguished themselves by their gallant leading.

Although not successful, the operation was most creditable to the fighting spirit of the Gordon Highlanders, most ably commanded by Major A. W. F. Baird, D.S.O.

As the 32nd French Division on the left had been unable to make any progress, the further advance of our infantry into the Wytschaete Wood was not practicable.

Possession of the western edge of the Petit Bois was, however, retained.

The ground was devoid of cover and so waterlogged that a rapid advance was impossible, the men sinking deep in the mud at every step they took.

The artillery throughout the day was very skilfully handled by the C.R.A.s of the 3rd, 4th and 5th Divisions: Major-General F. D. V. Wing, C.B., Brigadier-General G. F. Milne, C.B., D.S.O., and Brigadier-General J. E. W. Headlam, C.B., D.S.O.

The casualties during the day were about 17 officers and 407 other ranks. The losses of the enemy were very considerable, large numbers of dead being found in the Petit Bois and also in the communicating trenches in front of the Gordon Highlanders, in one of which a hundred were counted by a night patrol.

On this day the artillery of the 4th Division, 3rd Corps, was used in support of the attack, under orders of the General Officer Commanding 2nd Corps.

The remainder of the 3rd Corps made demonstrations against the enemy with a view to preventing him from detaching troops to the area of operations of the 2nd Corps.

From the 15th to the 17th December the offensive operations which were commenced on the 14th were continued, but were confined chiefly to artillery bombardment.

The infantry advance against Wytschaete Wood was not practicable until the French on our left could make some progress to afford protection to that flank.

On the 17th it was agreed that the plan of attack as arranged should be modified, but I was requested to continue demonstrations along my line in order to assist and support certain French operations which were being conducted elsewhere.

In his desire to act with energy up to his instructions to demonstrate and occupy the enemy, the General Officer Commanding the Indian Corps decided to take the advantage of what appeared to him a favourable opportunity to launch attacks against the advanced trenches in his front on the 18th and 19th December.

The attack of the Meerut Division on the left was made on the morning of the 19th with energy and determination, and was at first attended with considerable success, the enemy's advanced trenches being captured. Later on, however, a counter attack drove them back to their original position with considerable loss.

The attack of the Lahore Division commenced at 4.30 a.m. It was carried out by two companies each of the 1st Highland Light Infantry and the 1st Battalion, 4th Gurkha Rifles, of the Sirhind Brigade, under Lieutenant-Colonel R. W. H. Ronaldson. This attack was completely successful, two lines of the enemy's trenches being captured with little loss.

Before daylight the captured trenches were filled with as many men as they would hold. The front was very restricted, communication to the rear impossible.

At daybreak it was found that the position was practically untenable. Both flanks were in the air, and a supporting attack, which was late in starting, and, therefore, conducted during daylight, failed; although attempted with the greatest gallantry and resolution.

Lieutenant-Colonel Ronaldson held on till dusk, when the whole of the captured trenches had to be evacuated, and the detachment fell back to its original line.

By the night of the 19th December nearly all the ground gained during the day had been lost.

From daylight on the 20th December the enemy commenced a heavy fire from artillery and trench mortars on the whole front of the Indian Corps. This was followed by infantry attacks, which were in especial force against Givenchy, and between that place and La Quinque Rue.

At about 10 a.m. the enemy succeeded in driving back the Sirhind Brigade, and capturing a considerable part of Givenchy, but the 57th Rifles and 9th Bhopals, north of the canal, and the Connaught Rangers, south of it, stood firm.

The 15th Sikhs of the Divisional Reserve were already supporting the Sirhind Brigade. On the news of the retirement of the latter being received, the 47th Sikhs were also sent up to reinforce General Brunker. The 1st Manchester Regiment, 4th Suffolk Regiment, and two battalions of French Territorials under General Carnegy were ordered to launch a vigorous counter attack from Pont Fixe through Givenchy to retake by a flank attack the trenches lost by the Sirhind Brigade.

Orders were sent to General Carnegy to divert his attack on Givenchy Village, and to re-establish the situation there.

A battalion of the 58th French Division was sent to Annequin in support.

About 5 p.m. a gallant attack by the 1st Manchester Regiment and one company of the 4th Suffolk Regiment had captured Givenchy, and had cleared the enemy out of the two lines of trenches to the North-East. To the east of the village the 9th Bhopal Infantry and 57th Rifles had maintained their positions, but the enemy were still in possession of our trenches to the north of the village.

General Macbean, with the Secunderabad Cavalry Brigade, 2nd Battalion, 8th Gurkha Rifles, and the 47th Sikhs, was sent up to support General

Brunker, who at 2 p.m. directed General Macbean to move to a position of readiness in the second line trenches from Maris northward, and to counter-attack vigorously if opportunity offered.

Some considerable delay appears to have occurred, and it was not until 1 a.m. on the 21st that the 47th Sikhs and the 7th Dragoon Guards under the command of Lieutenant-Colonel H. A. Lemprière, D.S.O., of the latter regiment, were launched in counter-attack.

They reached the enemy's trenches, but were driven out by enfilade fire, their gallant Commander being killed.

The main attack by the remainder of General Macbean's force, with the remnants of Lieutenant-Colonel Lemprière's detachment (which had again been rallied), was finally pushed in at about 4.30 a.m., and also failed.

In the northern section of the defensive line the retirement of the 2nd Battalion, 2nd Gurkha Rifles, at about 10 a.m. on the 20th, had left the flank of the 1st Seaforth Highlanders, on the extreme right of the Meerut Division line, much exposed. This battalion was left shortly afterwards completely in the air by the retirement of the Sirhind Brigade.

The 58th Rifles, therefore, were ordered to support the left of the Seaforth Highlanders, to fill the gap created by the retirement of the Gurkhas.

During the whole of the afternoon strenuous efforts were made by the Seaforth Highlanders to clear the trenches to their right and left. The 1st

Battalion, 9th Gurkha Rifles, reinforced the 2nd Gurkhas near the orchard where the Germans were in occupation of the trenches abandoned by the latter regiment. The Garhwal Brigade was being very heavily attacked, and their trenches and loopholes were much damaged; but the brigade continued to hold its front and attack, connecting with the 6th Jats on the left of the Dehra Dun Brigade.

No advance in force was made by the enemy, but the troops were pinned to their ground by heavy artillery fire, the Seaforth Highlanders especially suffering heavily.

Shortly before nightfall the 2nd Royal Highlanders on the right of the Seaforth Highlanders had succeeded in establishing touch with the Sirhind Brigade; and the continuous line (though dented near the orchard) existed throughout the Meerut Division.

Early in the afternoon of December 20th orders were sent to the 1st Corps, which was then in general army reserve, to send an infantry brigade to support the Indian Corps.

The 1st Brigade was ordered to Béthune, and reached that place at midnight on 20th–21st December. Later in the day Sir Douglas Haig was ordered to move the whole of the 1st Division in support of the Indian Corps.

The 3rd Brigade reached Béthune between 8 a.m. and 9 a.m. on the 21st, and on the same date the 2nd Brigade arrived at Lacon at 1 p.m.

The 1st Brigade was directed on Givenchy, via

Pont Fixe, and the 3rd Brigade, through Gorre, on the trenches evacuated by the Sirhind Brigade.

The 2nd Brigade was directed to support; the Dehra Dun Brigade being placed at the disposal of the General Officer Commanding Meerut Division.

At 1 p.m. the General Officer Commanding 1st Division directed the 1st Brigade in attack from the west of Givenchy in a north-easterly direction, and the 3rd Brigade from Festubert in an east-north-easterly direction, the object being to pass the position originally held by us and to capture the German trenches 400 yards to the east of it.

By 5 p.m. the 1st Brigade had obtained a hold in Givenchy, and the ground south as far as the canal; and the 3rd Brigade had progressed to a point half a mile west of Festubert.

By nightfall the 1st South Wales Borderers and the 2nd Welsh Regiment of the 3rd Brigade had made a lodgment in the original trenches to the north-east of Festubert, the 1st Gloucestershire Regiment continuing the line southward along the track east of Festubert.

The 1st Brigade had established itself on the east side of Givenchy.

By 3 p.m. the 3rd Brigade was concentrated at Le Touret, and was ordered to retake the trenches which had been lost by the Dehra Dun Brigade.

By 10 p.m. the support trenches west of the orchard had been carried, but the original fire trenches had been so completely destroyed that they could not be occupied.

This operation was performed by the 1st Loyal North Lancashire Regiment and the 1st Northamptonshire Regiment, supported by the 2nd King's Royal Rifle Corps, in reserve.

Throughout this day the units of the Indian Corps rendered all the assistance and support they could in view of their exhausted condition.

At 1 p.m. on the 22nd Sir Douglas Haig took over command from Sir James Willcocks. The situation in the front line was then approximately as follows:—

South of the La Bassée Canal the Connaught Rangers of the Ferozepore Brigade had not been attacked. North of the canal a short length of our original line was still held by the 9th Bhopals and the 57th Rifles of the same brigade. Connecting with the latter was the 1st Brigade holding the village of Givenchy and its eastern and northern approaches. On the left of the 1st Brigade was the 3rd Brigade. Touch had been lost between the left of the former and the right of the latter. The 3rd Brigade held a line along, and in places advanced to, the east of the Festubert Road. Its left was in communication with the right of the Meerut Division line, where troops of the 2nd Brigade had just relieved the 1st Seaforth Highlanders. To the north, units of the 2nd Brigade held an indented line west of the orchard, connecting with half of the 2nd Royal Highlanders, half of the 41st Dogras and the 1st Battalion, 9th Gurkha Rifles. From this point to the north the 6th Jats and the whole of the Garhwal Brigade occupied the original line which they had held from the commencement of the operations.

The relief of most units of the southern sector was effected on the night of 22nd December. The Meerut Division remained under the orders of the 1st Corps, and was not completely withdrawn until the 27th December.

In the evening the position at Givenchy was practically reestablished, and the 3rd Brigade had re-occupied the old line of trenches.

During the 23rd the enemy's activities ceased, and the whole position was restored to very much its original condition.

In my last despatch I had occasion to mention the prompt and ready help I received from the Lahore Division, under the command of Major-General H. B. B. Watkis, C.B., which was thrown into action immediately on arrival, when the British Forces were very hard pressed during the battle of Ypres-Armentières.

The Indian troops have fought with the utmost steadfastness and gallantry whenever they have been called upon.

Weather conditions were abnormally bad, the snow and floods precluding any active operations during the first three weeks of January.

At 7.30 a.m. on the 25th January the enemy began to shell Béthune, and at 8 a.m. a strong hostile infantry attack developed south of the canal, preceded by a heavy bombardment of artillery, minenwerfers, and, possibly, the explosion of mines, though the latter is doubtful.

The British line south of the canal formed a pronounced salient from the canal on the left, thence running forward toward the railway triangle and back to the main La Bassée–Bethune Road, where it joined the French. This line was occupied by half a battalion of the Scots Guards, and half a battalion of the Coldstream Guards, of the 1st Infantry Brigade. The trenches in the salient were blown in almost at once; and the enemy's attack penetrated this line. Our troops retired to a partially prepared second line, running approximately due north and south from the canal to the road, some 500 yards west of the railway triangle. This second line had been strengthened by the construction of a keep half way between the canal and the road. Here the other two half battalions of the above-mentioned regiments were in support.

These supports held up the enemy who, however, managed to establish himself in the brick stacks and some communication trenches between the keep, the road and the canal—and even beyond the west of the keep on either side of it.

The London Scottish had in the meantime been sent up in support, and a counter-attack was organised with the 1st Royal Highlanders, part of the 1st Cameron Highlanders, and the 2nd King's Royal Rifle Corps, the latter regiment having been sent forward from the Divisional Reserve.

The counter-attack was delayed in order to synchronise with a counter-attack north of the canal which was arranged for 1 p.m.

At 1 p.m. these troops moved forward, their flanks making good progress near the road and the canal, but their centre being held up. The 2nd Royal Sussex Regiment was then sent forward, late in the afternoon, to reinforce. The result was that the Germans were driven back far enough to enable a somewhat broken line to be taken up, running from the culvert on the railway, almost due south to the keep, and thence south-east to the main road.

The French left near the road had also been attacked and driven back a little, but not to so great an extent as the British right. Consequently, the French left was in advance of the British right and exposed to a possible flank attack from the north.

The Germans did not, however, persevere further in their attack.

The above-mentioned line was strengthened during the night; and the 1st Guards Brigade, which had suffered severely, was withdrawn into reserve and replaced by the 2nd Infantry Brigade.

While this was taking place another, an equally severe attack was delivered north of the canal against the village of Givenchy.

At 8.15 a.m., after a heavy artillery bombardment with high explosive shells, the enemy's infantry advanced under the effective fire of our artillery, which, however, was hampered by the constant interruption of telephonic communication between the observers and batteries. Nevertheless, our artillery fire, combined with that of the infantry in the fire trenches, had the effect of driving the enemy from his original direction of advance, with the result that his troops crowded together on the north-east corner of the village and broke through into the centre of the village as far as the keep, which had been previously put in a state of defence. The Germans had lost heavily, and a well-timed local counter-attack, delivered by the reserves of the 2nd Welsh Regiment and 1st South Wales Borderers, and by a company of the 1st Royal Highlanders (lent by the 1st Brigade as a working party—this company was at work on the keep at the time), was completely successful, with the result that, after about an hour's street fighting, all who had broken into the village were either captured or killed; and the original line round the village was re-established by noon.

South of the village, however, and close to the canal, the right of the 2nd Royal Munster Fusiliers fell back in conformity with the troops south of the canal; but after dark that regiment moved forward and occupied the old line.

During the course of the attack on Givenchy the enemy made five assaults on the salient at the north-east of the village about French Farm, but was repulsed every time with heavy loss.

On the morning of the 29th January attacks were made on the right of the 1st Corps, south of the canal in the neighbourhood of La Bassée.

The enemy (part of the 14th German Corps), after a severe shelling, made a violent attack with scaling ladders on the keep, also to the north and south of it. In the keep and on the north side the Sussex Regiment held the enemy off, inflicting on him serious losses. On the south side the hostile infantry succeeded in reaching the Northamptonshire Regiment's trenches; but were immediately counter-attacked and all killed. Our artillery cooperated well with the infantry in repelling the attack.

In this action our casualties were inconsiderable, but the enemy lost severely, more than 200 of his killed alone being left in front, of our position.

On the 1st February a fine piece of work was carried out by the 4th Brigade in the neighbourhood of Cuinchy.

Some of the 2nd Coldstream Guards were driven from their trenches at 2.30 a.m., but made a stand some twenty yards east of them in a position which they held till morning.

A counter-attack, launched at 3.15 a.m. by one company of the Irish Guards and half a company of the 2nd Coldstream Guards, proved unsuccessful, owing to heavy rifle fire from the east and south.

At 10.05 a.m., acting under orders of the 1st Division, a heavy bombardment was opened on the lost ground for ten minutes; and this was followed immediately by an assault by about 50 men of the 2nd Coldstream Guards with bayonets, led by Captain A. Leigh Bennett, followed by 30 men of the Irish Guards, led by Second Lieutenant F. F. Graham, also with bayonets. These were followed by a party of Royal Engineers with sand bags and wire.

All the ground which had been lost was brilliantly retaken; the 2nd Coldstream Guards also taking another German trench and capturing two machine guns.

Thirty-two prisoners fell into our hands.

The General Officer Commanding 1st Division describes the preparation by the artillery as "splendid, the high explosive shells dropping in the exact spot with absolute precision."

In forwarding his report on this engagement, the General Officer Commanding First Army writes as follows:—

"Special credit is due—
(i) To Major-General Haking, Commanding 1st Division, for the prompt manner in which he arranged this counter-attack and for the general plan of action, which was crowned with success.
(ii) To the General Officer Commanding the 4th Brigade (Lord Cavan) for the thorough manner in which he carried out the orders of the General Officer Commanding the Division.
(iii) To the regimental officers, non-commissioned officers and men of the 2nd Coldstream Guards and Irish Guards, who, with indomitable pluck, stormed two sets of barricades, captured three German trenches, two machine guns, and killed or made prisoners many of the enemy."

During the period under report the Royal Flying Corps has again performed splendid service.

Although the weather was almost uniformly bad and the machines suffered from constant exposure, there have been only thirteen days on which no actual reconnaissance has been effected. Approximately, one hundred thousand miles have been flown.

In addition to the daily and constant work of reconnaissance and co-operation with the artillery, a number of aerial combats have been fought, raids carried out, detrainments harassed, parks and petrol depôts bombed, etc.

Various successful bomb-dropping raids have been carried out, usually against the enemy's aircraft material. The principle of attacking hostile aircraft whenever and wherever seen (unless highly important information is being delivered) has been adhered to, and has resulted in the moral fact that enemy machines invariably beat immediate retreat when chased.

Five German aeroplanes are known to have been brought to the ground, and it would appear probable that others, though they have managed to reach their own lines, have done so in a considerably damaged condition.

In my despatch of 20th November, 1914, I referred to the reinforcements of Territorial Troops which I had received, and I mentioned several units which had already been employed in the fighting line.

In the positions which I held for some years before the outbreak of this war I was brought into close contact with the Territorial Force, and I found every reason to hope and believe that, when the hour of trial arrived, they would justify every hope and trust which was placed in them.

The Lords Lieutenant of Counties and the Associations which worked under them bestowed a vast amount of labour and energy on the organization of the Territorial Force; and I trust it may be some recompense to them to know that I, and the principal Commanders serving under me, consider that the Territorial Force has far more than justified the most sanguine hopes that any of us ventured to entertain of their value and use in the field. Commanders of Cavalry Divisions are unstinted in their praise of the manner in which the Yeomanry regiments attached to their brigades have done their duty, both in and out of action. The service of Divisional Cavalry is now almost entirely performed by Yeomanry, and Divisional Commanders report that they are very efficient.

Army Corps Commanders are loud in their praise of the Territorial Battalions which form part of nearly all the brigades at the front in the first line, and more than one of them have told me that these battalions are fast approaching—if they have not already reached—the standard of efficiency of Regular Infantry.

I wish to add a word about the Officers Training Corps. The presence of the Artists' Rifles

(28th Battalion, The London Regiment) with the Army in France enabled me also to test the value of this organization.

Having had some experience in peace of the working of the Officers Training Corps, I determined to turn the Artists' Rifles (which formed part of the Officers Training Corps in peace time) to its legitimate use. I therefore established the battalion as a Training Corps for Officers in the field.

The cadets pass through a course, which includes some thoroughly practical training as all cadets do a tour of 48 hours in the trenches, and afterwards write a report on what they see and notice. They also visit an observation post of a battery or group of batteries, and spend some hours there.

A Commandant has been appointed, and he arranges and supervises the work, sets schemes for practice, administers the school, delivers lectures, and reports on the candidates.

The cadets are instructed in all branches of military training suitable for platoon commanders.

Machine gun tactics, a knowledge of which is so necessary for all junior officers, is a special feature of the course of instruction.

When first started the school was able to turn out officers at the rate of 75 a month. This has since been increased to 100.

Reports received from Divisional and Army Corps Commanders on officers who have been trained at the school are most satisfactory.

Since the date of my last report I have been able to make a close personal inspection of all the units in the command. I was most favourably impressed by all I saw.

The troops composing the Army in France have been subjected to as severe a trial as it is possible to impose upon any body of men. The desperate fighting described in my last despatch had hardly been brought to a conclusion when they were called upon to face the rigours and hardships of a winter campaign. Frost and snow have alternated with periods of continuous rain.

The men have been called upon to stand for many hours together almost up to their waists in bitterly cold water, only separated by one or two hundred yards from a most vigilant enemy.

Although every measure which science and medical knowledge could suggest to mitigate these hardships was employed, the sufferings of the men have been very great.

In spite of all this they presented, at the inspections to which I have referred, a most soldier-like, splendid, though somewhat war-worn appearance. Their spirit remains high and confident; their general health is excellent, and their condition most satisfactory.

I regard it as most unfortunate that circumstances have prevented any account of many splendid instances of courage and endurance, in the face of almost unparalleled hardship and fatigue in war, coming regularly to the knowledge of the public.

Reinforcements have arrived from England with remarkable promptitude and rapidity. They have been speedily drafted into the ranks, and most of the units I inspected were nearly complete when I saw them. In appearance and quality the drafts sent out have exceeded my most sanguine expectations, and I consider the Army in France is much indebted to the Adjutant-General's Department at the War Office for the efficient manner in which its requirements have been met in this most essential respect.

With regard to these inspections, I may mention in particular the fine appearance presented by the 27th and 28th Divisions, composed principally of battalions which had come from India. Included in the former division was the Princess Patricia's Royal Canadian Regiment. They are a magnificent set of men, and have since done excellent work in the trenches.

It was some three weeks after the events recorded that I made my inspection of the Indian Corps, under Sir James Willcocks. The appearance they presented was most satisfactory, and fully confirmed my first opinion that the Indian troops only required rest, and a little acclimatizing, to bring out all their fine inherent fighting qualities.

I saw the whole of the Indian Cavalry Corps, under Lieutenant-General Rimington, on a mounted parade soon after their arrival. They are a magnificent body of Cavalry, and will, I feel sure, give the best possible account of themselves when called upon.

In the meantime, at their own particular request, they have taken their turn in the trenches and performed most useful and valuable service.

The Rt. Rev. Bishop Taylor Smith, C.V.O., D.D., Chaplain-General to the Forces, arrived at my Headquarters on 6th January, on a tour of inspection throughout the command.

The Cardinal Archbishop of Westminster has also visited most of the Irish Regiments at the front and the principal centres on the Line of Communications.

In a quiet and unostentatious manner the chaplains of all denominations have worked with devotion and energy in their respective spheres.

The number with the forces in the field at the commencement of the war was comparatively small, but towards the end of last year the Rev. J. M. Simms, D.D., K.H.C., Principal Chaplain, assisted by his Secretary, the Rev. W. Drury, reorganised the branch, and placed the spiritual welfare of the soldier on a more satisfactory footing. It is hoped that the further increase of personnel may be found possible.

I cannot speak too highly of the devoted manner in which all chaplains, whether with the troops in the trenches, or in attendance on the sick and wounded in casualty clearing stations and hospitals on the line of communications, have worked throughout the campaign.

Since the commencement of hostilities the work of the Royal Army Medical Corps has been carried out with untiring zeal, skill and devotion. Whether at the front under conditions such as obtained during the fighting on the Aisne, when casualties were heavy and accommodation for their reception had to be improvised, or on the line of communications, where an average of some 11,000 patients have been daily under treatment, the organisation of the Medical Services has always been equal to the demands made upon it.

The careful system of sanitation introduced into the Army has, with the assistance of other measures, kept the troops free from any epidemic, in support of which it is to be noticed that since the commencement of the war some 500 cases only of enteric have occurred.

The organisation for the first time in war of Motor Ambulance Convoys is due to the initiative and organising powers of Surgeon-General T. J. O'Donnell, D.S.O., ably assisted by Major P Evans, Royal Army Medical Corps.

Two of these convoys, composed entirely of Red Cross Society personnel, have done excellent work under the superintendence of Regular Medical Officers.

Twelve Hospital Trains ply between the front and the various bases. I have visited several of the trains when halted in stations, and have found them conducted with great comfort and efficiency.

During the more recent phase of the campaign the creation of Rest Depôts at the front has materially reduced the wastage of men to the Line of Communications.

Since the latter part of October, 1914, the whole of the medical arrangements have been in the hands of Surgeon-General Sir A. T. Sloggett, C.M.G., K.H.S., under whom Surgeon-General T. P. Woodhouse and Surgeon-General T. J. O'Donnell have been responsible for the organisation on the Line of Communications and at the front respectively.

The exceptional and peculiar conditions brought about by the weather have caused large demands to be made upon the resources and skill of the Royal Engineers.

Every kind of expedient has had to be thought out and adopted to keep the lines of trenches and defence work effective.

The Royal Engineers have shown themselves as capable of overcoming the ravages caused by violent rain and floods as they have been throughout in neutralising the effect of the enemy's artillery.

In this connection I wish particularly to mention the excellent services performed by my Chief Engineer, Brigadier-General G. H. Fowke, who has been indefatigable in supervising all such work. His ingenuity and skill have been most valuable in the local construction of the various expedients which experience has shown to be necessary in prolonged trench warfare.

I have no reason to modify in any material degree my views of the general military situation, as expressed in my despatch of November 20th, 1914.

I have once more gratefully to acknowledge the valuable help and support I have received throughout this period from General Foch, General D'Urbal and General Maud'huy of the French Army.

I have the honour to be,
Your Lordship's most obedient Servant,
J. D. P. FRENCH,
Field–Marshal,Commanding–in–Chief,
The British Army in the Field.

MILITARY DESPATCH
DATED
5th April, 1915

PUBLISHED IN THE SUPPLEMENT TO THE "LONDON
GAZETTE", NO. 29128, OF 14TH APRIL, 1915.

From The Field-Marshal Commanding-in-Chief,
the British Army in the Field to the Secretary of State
for War, War Office, London, S.W.

General Headquarters, 5*th April*, 1915.

MY LORD,

I have the honour to report the operations of the Forces under my command since the date of my last despatch, 2nd February, 1915.

The event of chief interest and importance which has taken place is the victory achieved over the enemy at the Battle of Neuve Chapelle, which was fought on the 10th, 11th and 12th of March. The main attack was delivered by troops of the First Army under the command of General Sir Douglas Haig, supported by a large force of Heavy Artillery, a Division of Cavalry and some Infantry of the general reserve.

Secondary and holding attacks and demonstrations were made along the front of the Second Army under the direction of its Commander, General Sir Horace Smith-Dorrien.

Whilst the success attained was due to the magnificent bearing and indomitable courage displayed by the troops of the 4th and Indian Corps, I consider that the able and skilful dispositions which were made by the General Officer Commanding First Army contributed largely to the defeat of the enemy and to the capture of his position. The energy and vigour with which General Sir Douglas Haig handled his command show him to be a leader of great ability and power.

Another action of considerable importance was brought about by a surprise attack of the Germans made on the 14th March against the 27th Division holding the trenches east of St. Eloi. A large force of artillery was concentrated in this area under cover of mist, and a heavy volume of fire was suddenly brought to bear on the trenches at 5 p.m. This artillery attack was accompanied by two mine explosions; and, in the confusion caused by these and the suddenness of the attack, the position of St. Eloi was captured and held for some hours by the enemy.

Well directed and vigorous counter attacks, in which the troops of the 5th Army Corps showed great bravery and determination, restored the situation by the evening of the 15th.

A more detailed account of these operations will appear in subsequent pages of this despatch.

On the 6th February a brilliant action by troops of the 1st Corps materially improved our position in the area south of the La Bassée Canal. During the previous night parties of Irish Guards and of the 3rd Battalion Coldstream Guards had succeeded in gaining ground whence converging fire could be directed on the flanks and rear of certain "brickstacks" occupied by the Germans, which had been for some time a source of considerable annoyance.

At 2 p.m. the affair commenced with a severe bombardment of the "brickstacks" and the enemy trenches. A brisk attack by the 3rd Coldstream Guards and Irish Guards from our trenches west of the "brickstacks" followed, and was supported by fire from the flanking positions which had been seized the previous night by the same regiments. The attack succeeded, the "brickstacks" were occupied without difficulty, and a line established north and south through a point about forty yards east of the "brickstacks."

The casualties suffered by the 5th Corps throughout the period under review, and particularly during the month of February, have been heavier than those in other parts of the line. I regret this; but I do not think, taking all the circumstances into consideration, that they were unduly numerous. The position then occupied by the 5th Corps has always been a very vulnerable part of our line; the ground is marshy, and trenches are most difficult to construct and maintain. The 27th and 28th Divisions of the 5th Corps have had no previous experience of European warfare, and a number of the units composing it had only recently returned from service in tropical climates. In consequence, the hardships of a rigorous winter campaign fell with greater weight upon these Divisions than upon any other in the command.

Chiefly owing to these causes, the 5th Corps, up to the beginning of March, was constantly engaged in counter-attacks to retake trenches and ground which had been lost.

In their difficult and arduous task, however, the troops displayed the utmost gallantry and devotion; and it is most creditable to the skill and energy of their leaders that I am able to report how well they have surmounted all their difficulties, that the ground first taken over by them is still intact, and held with little greater loss than is incurred by troops in all other parts of the line.

On the 14th February the 82nd Brigade of the 27th Division was driven from its trenches east of St. Eloi; but by 7 a.m. on the 15th all these trenches had been recaptured, fifteen prisoners taken, and sixty German dead counted in front of the trenches. Similarly in the 28th Division trenches were lost by the 85th Brigade and retaken the following night.

During the month of February the enemy made several attempts to get through all along the line, but he was invariably repulsed with loss. A particularly vigorous attempt was made on the 17th February against the trenches held by the Indian Corps, but it was brilliantly repulsed.

On February 28th a successful minor attack was made on the enemy's trenches near St. Eloi by small parties of the Princess Patricia's Canadian Light Infantry. The attack was divided into three small groups, the whole under the command of Lieutenant Crabbe: No. 1 Group under Lieutenant Papineau, No. 2 Group under Sergeant Patterson, and No. 3 Group under Company Sergeant-Major Lloyd.

The head of the party got within fifteen or twenty yards of the German trench and charged; it was dark at the time (about 5.15 a.m.).

Lieutenant Crabbe, who showed the greatest dash and *élan*, took his party over everything in the trench until they had gone down it about eighty yards, when they were stopped by a barricade of sandbags and timber. This party, as well as the others, then pulled down the front face of the German parapet. A number of Germans were killed and wounded, and a few prisoners were taken.

The services performed by this distinguished corps have continued to be very valuable since I had occasion to refer to them in my last despatch. They have been most ably organised, trained and commanded by Lieutenant-Colonel F. D. Farquhar, D.S.O., who, I deeply regret to say, was killed while superintending some trench work on the 20th March. His loss will be deeply felt.

A very gallant attack was made by the 4th Battalion of the King's Royal Rifle Corps of the 80th Brigade on the enemy's trenches in the early hours of March 2nd. The Battalion was led by Major Widdrington, who launched it at 12.30 a.m. (he himself being wounded during its progress), covered by an extremely accurate and effective artillery fire. About sixty yards of the enemy's trench were cleared, but the attack was brought to a standstill by a strong barricade, in attempting to storm which several casualties were incurred.

During the month of February I arranged with General Foch to render the 9th French Corps, holding the trenches on my left, some much-needed rest by sending the three Divisions of the British Cavalry Corps to hold a portion of the French trenches, each division for a period of ten days alternately.

It was very gratifying to me to note once again in this campaign the eager readiness which the Cavalry displayed to undertake a rôle which does not properly belong to them in order to support and assist their French comrades.

In carrying out this work leaders, officers and men displayed the same skill and energy which I have had reason to comment upon in former despatches.

The time passed by the Cavalry in the French trenches was, on the whole, quiet and uneventful, but there are one or two incidents calling for remark.

At about 1.45 a.m. on 16th February a half-hearted attack was made against the right of the line held by the 2nd Cavalry Division, but it was easily repulsed by rifle fire, and the enemy left several dead in front of the trenches. The attack was delivered against the second and third trenches from the right of the line of this Division.

At 6 a.m. on the 21st the enemy blew up one of the 2nd Cavalry Division trenches, held by the 16th Lancers, and some adjoining French trenches. The enemy occupied forty yards of our trench and tried to advance, but were stopped. An immediate counter-attack by the supporting squadron was stopped by machine-gun fire. The line was established opposite the gap, and a counter-attack by two squadrons and one company of French reserve was ordered. At 5.30 p.m. 2nd Cavalry Division reported that the counter-attack did not succeed in retaking the trench blown in, but that a new line had been established forty yards in rear of it, and that there was no further activity on the part of the enemy. At 10 p.m. the situation was unchanged.

The Commander of the Indian Cavalry Corps expressed a strong desire that the troops under his command should gain some experience in trench warfare. Arrangements were made, therefore, with the General Officer Commanding the Indian Corps, in pursuance of which the various units of the Indian Cavalry Corps have from time to time taken a turn in the trenches, and have thereby gained some valuable experience.

About the end of February many vital considerations induced me to believe that a vigorous offensive movement by the Forces under my command should be planned and carried out at the earliest possible moment.

Amongst the more important reasons which convinced me of this necessity were:—The general aspect of the Allied situation throughout Europe, and particularly the marked success of the Russian Army in repelling the violent onslaughts of Marshal Von Hindenburg; the apparent weakening of the enemy in my front, and the necessity for assisting our Russian Allies to the utmost by holding as many hostile troops as possible in the Western Theatre; the efforts to this end which were being made by the French Forces at Arras and Champagne; and, perhaps the most weighty consideration of all, the need of fostering the offensive spirit in the troops under my command after the trying and possibly enervating experiences which they had gone through of a severe winter in the trenches.

In a former despatch I commented upon the difficulties and drawbacks which the winter weather in this climate imposes upon a vigorous offensive. Early

in March these difficulties became greatly lessened by
the drying up of the country and by spells of brighter
weather.

I do not propose in this despatch to enter at
length into the considerations which actuated me in
deciding upon the plan, time and place of my attack,
but Your Lordship is fully aware of these.

As mentioned above, the main attack was carried
out by units of the First Army, supported by troops of
the Second Army and the general reserve.

The object of the main attack was to be the capture of the village of Neuve Chapelle and the enemy's
position at that point, and the establishment of our
line as far forward as possible to the east of that place.

The object, nature and scope of the attack, and
instructions for the conduct of the operation were
communicated by me to Sir Douglas Haig in a secret
memorandum dated 19th February.

The main topographical feature of this part of the
theatre is a marked ridge which runs south-west from
a point two miles south-west of Lille to the village of
Fournes, whence two spurs run out, one due west to
a height known as Haut Pommereau, the other following the line of the main road to Illies.

The buildings of the village of Neuve Chapelle
run along the Rue du Bois-Fauquissart Road. There is
a triangle of roads just north of the village. This area
consists of a few big houses, with walls, gardens,
orchards, etc., and here, with the aid of numerous
machine guns, the enemy had established a strong
post which flanked the approaches to the village.

The Bois du Biez, which lies roughly south-east of the village of Neuve Chapelle, influenced the course of this operation.

Full instructions as to assisting and supporting the attack were issued to the Second Army.

The battle opened at 7.30 a.m. on the 10th March by a powerful artillery bombardment of the enemy's position at Neuve Chapelle. The artillery bombardment had been well prepared and was most effective, except on the extreme northern portion of the front of attack.

At 8.05 a.m. the 23rd (left) and 25th (right) Brigades of the 8th Division assaulted the German trenches on the north-west of the village.

At the same hour the Garhwal Brigade of the Meerut Division, which occupied the position to the south of Neuve Chapelle, assaulted the German trenches in its front.

The Garhwal Brigade and the 25th Brigade carried the enemy's lines of entrenchments where the wire entanglements had been almost entirely swept away by our shrapnel fire. The 23rd Brigade, however, on the north-east, was held up by the wire entanglements, which were not sufficiently cut.

At 8.05 a.m. the artillery turned on to Neuve Chapelle, and at 8.35 a.m. the advance of the infantry was continued.

The 25th and Garwhal Brigades pushed on eastward and north-eastward respectively, and succeeded in getting a footing in the village. The 23rd Brigade was still held up in front of the enemy's wire entanglements, and could not progress. Heavy losses were suffered, especially in the Middlesex Regiment and the Scottish Rifles. The progress, however, of the 25th Brigade into Neuve Chapelle immediately to the south of the 23rd Brigade had the effect of turning the southern flank of the enemy's defences in front of the 23rd Brigade.

This fact, combined with powerful artillery support, enabled the 23rd Brigade to get forward between 10 and 11 a.m., and by 11 a.m. the whole of the village of Neuve Chapelle and the roads leading northward and south-westward from the eastern end of that village were in our hands.

During this time our artillery completely cut off the village and the surrounding country from any German reinforcements which could be thrown into the fight to restore the situation by means of a curtain of shrapnel fire. Prisoners subsequently reported that all attempts at reinforcing the front line were checked. Steps were at once taken to consolidate the position won.

Considerable delay occurred after the capture of the Neuve Chapelle position. The infantry was greatly disorganised by the violent nature of the attack and by its passage through the enemy's trenches and the buildings of the village. It was necessary to gets units to some extent together before pushing on. The telephonic communication being cut by the enemy's fire rendered communication between front and rear most difficult. The fact of the left of the 23rd Brigade having been held up had kept back the 8th

Division, and had involved a portion of the 25th Brigade in fighting to the north out of its proper direction of advance. All this required adjustment. An orchard held by the enemy north of Neuve Chapelle also threatened the flank of an advance towards the Aubers Ridge.

I am of opinion that this delay would not have occurred had the clearly expressed order of the General Officer Commanding First Army been more carefully observed. The difficulties above enumerated might have been overcome at an earlier period of the day if the General Officer Commanding 4th Corps had been able to bring his reserve brigades more speedily into action. As it was, the further advance did not commence before 3.30 p.m.

The 21st Brigade was able to form up in the open on the left without a shot being fired at it, thus showing that at the time the enemy's resistance had been paralysed. The Brigade pushed forward in the direction of Moulin de Pietre.

At first it made good progress, but was subsequently held up by the machine-gun fire from the houses and from a defended work in the line of the German entrenchments opposite the right of the 22nd Brigade.

Further to the south the 24th Brigade, which had been directed on Pietre, was similarly held up by machine-guns in the houses and trenches at the road junction six hundred yards north-west of Pietre.

The 25th Brigade, on the right of the 24th, was also held up by machine-guns from a bridge held by the Germans, over the River des Layes, which is situated to the north-west of the Bois du Biez.

Whilst two Brigades of the Meerut Division were establishing themselves on the new line, the Dehra Dun Brigade, supported by the Jullundur Brigade of the Lahore Division, moved to the attack of the Bois du Biez, but were held up on the line of the River des Layes by the German post at the bridge which enfiladed them and brought them to a standstill.

The defended bridge over the River des Layes and its neighbourhood immediately assumed considerable importance. Whilst artillery fire was brought to bear, as far as circumstances would permit, on this point, Sir Douglas Haig directed the 1st Corps to despatch one or more battalions of the 1st Brigade in support of the troops attacking the bridge. Three battalions were thus sent to Richebourg St. Vaast. Darkness coming on, and the enemy having brought up reinforcements, no further progress could be made, and the Indian Corps and 4th Corps proceeded to consolidate the position they had gained.

Whilst the operations which I have thus briefly recorded were going on, the 1st Corps in accordance with orders, delivered an attack in the morning from Givenchy, simultaneously with that against Neuve Chapelle; but as the enemy's wire was insufficiently cut, very little progress could be made, and the troops at this point did little more than hold fast the Germans in front of them.

On the following day, March 11th, the attack was renewed by the 4th and Indian Corps, but it was soon seen that a further advance would be impossible until the artillery had dealt effectively with the various houses and defended localities which held up the troops along the entire front. Efforts were made to direct the artillery fire accordingly; but owing to the weather conditions, which did not permit of aerial observation, and the fact that nearly all the telephonic communications between the artillery observers and their batteries had been cut, it was impossible to do so with sufficient accuracy. Even when our troops which were pressing forward occupied a house here and there, it was not possible to stop our artillery fire, and the infantry had to be withdrawn.

The two principal points which barred the advance were the same as on the preceding day— namely, the enemy's position about Moulin de Pietre and at the bridge over the River des Layes.

On the 12th March the same unfavourable conditions as regards weather prevailed, and hampered artillery action.

Although the 4th and Indian Corps most gallantly attempted to capture the strongly fortified positions in their front, they were unable to maintain themselves, although they succeeded in holding them for some hours.

Operations on this day were chiefly remarkable for the violent counter-attacks, supported by artillery, which were delivered by the Germans, and the ease with which they were repulsed.

As most of the objects for which the operations had been undertaken had been attained and as there were reasons why I considered it inadvisable to continue the attack at that time, I directed Sir Douglas Haig on the night of the 12th to hold and consolidate the ground which had been gained by the 4th and Indian Corps, and to suspend further offensive operations for the present.

On the morning of the 12th I informed the General Officer Commanding 1st Army that he could call on the 2nd Cavalry Division, under General Gough, for immediate support in the event of the successes of the First Army opening up opportunities for its favourable employment. This Division and a Brigade of the North Midland Division, which was temporarily attached to it, was moved forward for this purpose.

The 5th Cavalry Brigade, under Sir Philip Chetwode, reached the Rue Bacquerot at 4 p.m., with a view to rendering immediate support; but he was informed by the General Officer Commanding 4th Corps that the situation was not so favourable as he had hoped it would be, and that no further action by the cavalry was advisable.

General Gough's command, therefore, retired to Estaires.

The artillery of all kinds was handled with the utmost energy and skill, and rendered invaluable support in the prosecution of the attack.

The losses during these three days' fighting were, I regret to say, very severe, numbering—

190 officers and 2,337 other ranks, killed.
359 officers and 8,174 other ranks, wounded.
23 officers and 1,728 other ranks, missing.

But the results attained were, in my opinion, wide and far reaching.

The enemy left several thousand dead on the battlefield which were seen and counted; and we have positive information that upwards of 12,000 wounded were removed to the north-east and east by train.

Thirty officers and 1,657 other ranks of the enemy were captured.

I can best express my estimate of this battle by quoting an extract from a Special Order of the Day which I addressed to Sir Douglas Haig and the First Army at its conclusion:—

> "I am anxious to express to you personally my warmest appreciation of the skilful manner in which you have carried out your orders, and my fervent and most heartfelt appreciation of the magnificent gallantry and devoted, tenacious courage displayed by all ranks whom you have ably led to success and victory."

Some operations in the nature of holding attacks, carried out by troops of the Second Army, were instrumental in keeping the enemy in front of them occupied, and preventing reinforcements being sent from those portions of the front to the main point of attack.

At 12.30 a.m. on the 12th March the 17th Infantry Brigade of the 4th Division, 3rd Corps, engaged in an attack on the enemy which resulted in the capture of the village of L'Epinette and adjacent farms.

Supported by a brisk fire from the 18th Infantry Brigade, the 17th Infantry Brigade, detailed for the attack, assaulted in two columns converging, and obtained the first houses of the village without much loss. The remainder of the village was very heavily wired, and the enemy got away by means of communication trenches while our men were cutting through the wire.

The enemy suffered considerable loss; our casualties being 5 officers and 30 other ranks, killed and wounded.

The result of this operation was that an advance of 300 yards was made on a front of half a mile.

All attempts to retake this position have been repulsed with heavy loss to the enemy.

The General Officer Commanding the Second Corps arranged for an attack on a part of the enemy's position to the south-west of the village of Wytschaete which he had timed to commence at 10 a.m. on the 12th March. Owing to dense fog, the assault could not be made until 4 o'clock in the afternoon. It was then commenced by the Wiltshire and Worcestershire Regiments, but was so hampered by the mist and the approach of darkness that nothing more was effected than holding the enemy to his ground.

The action of St. Eloi referred to in the first paragraph of this despatch commenced at 5 p.m. on the 14th March by a very heavy cannonade which was directed against our trenches in front of St. Eloi, the village itself and the approaches to it. There is a large mound lying to the south-east of the village. When the artillery attack was at its height a mine was exploded under this mound, and a strong hostile infantry attack was immediately launched against the trenches and the mound.

Our artillery opened fire at once, as well as our infantry, and inflicted considerable losses on the enemy during their advance; but, chiefly owing to the explosion of the mine and the surprise of the overwhelming artillery attack, the enemy's infantry had penetrated the first line of trenches at some points. As a consequence the garrisons of other works which had successfully resisted the assault were enfiladed and forced to retire just before it turned dark.

A counter attack was at once organised by the General Officer Commanding 82nd Brigade, under the orders of the General Officer Commanding 27th Division, who brought up a reserve brigade to support it.

The attack was launched at 2 a.m., and the 82nd Brigade succeeded in recapturing the portion of the village of St. Eloi which was in the hands of the enemy and a portion of the trenches east of it. At 3 a.m. the 80th Brigade in support took more trenches to the east and west of the village. The counter attack, which was well carried out under difficult conditions, resulted in the recapture of all lost ground of material importance.

It is satisfactory to be able to record that, though the troops occupying the first line of trenches were at first overwhelmed, they afterwards behaved very gallantly in the counter-attack for the recovery of the lost ground; and the following units earned and received the special commendation of the Army Commander:—The 2nd Royal Irish Fusiliers, the 2nd Duke of Cornwall's Light Infantry, the 1st Leinster Regiment, the 4th Rifle Brigade and the Princess Patricia's Canadian Light Infantry.

A vigorous attack made by the enemy on the 17th to recapture these trenches was repulsed with great loss.

Throughout the period under review night enterprises by smaller or larger patrols, which were led with consummate skill and daring, have been very active along the whole line.

A moral superiority has thus been established, and valuable information has been collected.

I cannot speak too highly of the invincible courage and the remarkable resource displayed by these patrols.

The troops of the 3rd Corps have particularly impressed me by their conduct of these operations.

The work of the Royal Flying Corps throughout this period, and especially during the operations of the 10th, 11th, and 12th March, was of the greatest value. Though the weather on March 10th and on the subsequent days was very unfavourable for aerial work, on account of low-lying clouds and mist, a remarkable number of hours flying of a most valuable character were effected, and continuous and close reconnaissance was maintained over the enemy's front.

In addition to the work of reconnaissance and observation of artillery fire, the Royal Flying Corps was charged with the special duty of hampering the enemy's movements by destroying various points on his communications. The railways at Menin, Courtrai, Don and Douai were attacked, and it is known that very extensive damage was effected at certain of these places. Part of a troop train was hit by a bomb, a wireless installation near Lille is believed to have been effectively destroyed, and a house in which the enemy had installed one of his Headquarters was set on fire. These afford other instances of successful operations of this character. Most of the objectives mentioned were attacked at a height of only 100 to 150 feet. In one case the pilot descended to about 50 feet above the point he was attacking.

Certain new and important forms of activity, which it is undesirable to specify, have been initiated and pushed forward with much vigour and success.

There have been only eight days during the period under review on which reconnaissances have not been made. A total of approximately 130,000 miles have been flown—almost entirely over the enemy's lines.

No great activity has been shown over our troops on the part of the enemy's aircraft, but they have been attacked whenever and wherever met with, and usually forced down or made to seek refuge in their own lines.

In my last despatch I referred to the remarkable promptitude and rapidity with which reinforcements arrived in this country from England. In connection with this it is of interest to call attention to the fact that, in spite of the heavy casualties incurred in the fighting between the 10th and 15th March, all deficiencies, both in officers and rank and file, were made good within a few days of the conclusion of the battle.

The drafts for the Indian Contingents have much improved of late, and are now quite satisfactory.

Since the date of my last report the general health of the Army has been excellent; enteric has decreased, and there has been no recurrence on any appreciable scale of the "foot" trouble which appeared so threatening in December and January.

These results are due to the skill and energy which have characterised in a marked degree the work of the Royal Army Medical Corps throughout the campaign, under the able supervision of Surgeon-General T. J. O'Donnell, D.S.O., Deputy Director-General, Medical Services. But much credit is also due to Divisional, Brigade, Regimental and Company Commanders for the close supervision which has been kept over the health of their men by seeing that the precautions laid down for the troops before entering and after leaving the trenches are duly observed, and by the establishment and efficient maintenance of bathing-places and wash-houses, and by the ingenious means universally employed throughout the Forces to maintain the cleanliness of the men, having regard both to their bodies and their clothing.

I have inspected most of these houses and establishments, and consider them models of careful organisation and supervision.

I would particularly comment upon the energy displayed by the Royal Army Medical Corps in the scientific efforts they have made to discover and check disease in its earliest stages by a system of experimental research, which I think has never before been so fully developed in the field.

In this work they have been ably assisted by those distinguished members of the medical profession who are now employed as Military Medical Officers, and whose invaluable services I gratefully acknowledge.

The actual strength of the Force in the field has been increased and the health of the troops improved by a system of "convalescent" hospitals.

In these establishments slight wounds and minor ailments are treated, and men requiring attention and rest are received.

By these means efficient soldiers, whose services would otherwise be lost for a long time, are kept in the country, whilst a large number of men are given immediate relief and rest when they require it without removing them from the area of operations. This adds materially to the fighting efficiency of the Forces.

The principal convalescent hospital is at St. Omer. It was started and organised by Colonel A. F. L. Bate, Army Medical Service, whose zeal, energy, and organising power have rendered it a model hospital of its kind, and this example has materially assisted in the efficient organisation of similar smaller establishments at every Divisional Headquarters.

I have already commented upon the number and severity of the casualties in action which have occurred in the period under report. Here once again I have to draw attention to the excellent work done by Surgeon-General O'Donnell and his officers. No organisation could excel the efficiency of the arrangements—whether in regard to time, space, care and comfort, or transport—which are made for the speedy evacuation of the wounded.

I wish particularly to express my deep sense of the loss incurred by the Army in General, and by the Forces in France in particular, in the death of Brigadier-General J. E. Gough, V.C., C.M.G., A.D.C., late Brigadier-General, General Staff, First Army, which occurred on 22nd February as a result of a severe wound received on the 20th February when inspecting the trenches of the 4th Corps.

I always regarded General Gough as one of our most promising military leaders of the future. His services as a Staff Officer throughout the campaign have been invaluable, and I had already brought his name before Your Lordship for immediate promotion.

I can well understand how deeply these casualties are felt by the nation at large, but each daily report shows clearly that they are being endured on at least an equal scale by all the combatants engaged throughout Europe, friends and foes alike.

In war as it is to-day between civilised nations, armed to the teeth with the present deadly rifle and machine-gun, heavy casualties are absolutely unavoidable. For the slightest undue exposure the heaviest toll is exacted.

The power of defence conferred by modern weapons is the main cause of the long duration of the battles of the present day, and it is this fact which mainly accounts for such loss and waste of life.

Both one and the other can, however, be shortened and lessened if attacks can be supported by the most efficient and powerful force of artillery available; but an almost unlimited supply of ammunition is necessary and a most liberal discretionary power as to its use must be given to the Artillery Commanders.

I am confident that this is the only means by which great results can be obtained with a minimum of loss.

On the 15th February the Canadian Division began to arrive in this country. I inspected the Division, which was under the command of

Lieutenant-General E. A. H. Alderson, C.B., on 20th February.

They presented a splendid and most soldier-like appearance on parade. The men were of good physique, hard and fit. I judged by what I saw of them that they were well trained, and quite able to take their places in the line of battle.

Since then the Division has thoroughly justified the good opinion I formed of it.

The troops of the Canadian Division were first attached for a few days by brigades for training in the 3rd Corps trenches under Lieutenant-General Sir William Pulteney, who gave me such an excellent report of their efficiency that I was able to employ them in the trenches early in March.

During the Battle of Neuve Chapelle they held a part of the line allotted to the First Army, and, although they were not actually engaged in the main attack, they rendered valuable help by keeping the enemy actively employed in front of their trenches.

All the soldiers of Canada serving in the Army under my command have so far splendidly upheld the traditions of the Empire, and will, I feel sure, prove to be a great source of additional strength to the forces in this country.

In former despatches I have been able to comment very favourably upon the conduct and bearing of the Territorial Forces throughout the operations in which they have been engaged. As time goes on, and I see more and more of their work, whether in the trenches or engaged in more active operations, I am still further impressed with their value.

Several battalions were engaged in the most critical moments of the heavy fighting which occurred in the middle of March, and they acquitted themselves with the utmost credit.

Up till lately the troops of the Territorial Force in this country were only employed by battalions, but for some weeks past I have seen formed divisions working together, and I have every hope that their employment in the larger units will prove as successful as in the smaller.

These opinions are fully borne out by the result of the close inspection which I have recently made of the North Midland Division, under Major-General Hon. Montague-Stuart-Wortley, and the 2nd London Division, under Major-General Barter.

General Baron Von Kaulbars, of the Russian General Staff, arrived at my Headquarters on the 18th March. He was anxious to study our aviation system, and I gave him every opportunity of doing so.

The Bishop of London arrived here with his Chaplain on Saturday, March 27th, and left on Monday, April 5th.

During the course of his visit to the Army His Lordship was at the front every day, and I think I am right in saying that there was scarcely a unit in the command which was not at one time or another present at his services or addresses. Personal fatigue and even danger were completely ignored by His

Lordship. The Bishop held several services virtually under shell fire, and it was with difficulty that he could be prevented from carrying on his ministrations under rifle fire in the trenches.

I am anxious to place on record my deep sense of the good effect produced throughout the Army by this self-sacrificing devotion on the part of the Bishop of London, to whom I feel personally very deeply indebted.

I have once more to remark upon the devotion to duty, courage and contempt of danger which has characterised the work of the Chaplains of the Army throughout this campaign.

The increased strength of the Force and the gradual exhaustion of the local resources have necessitated a corresponding increase in our demands on the Line of Communications, since we are now compelled to import many articles which in the early stages could be obtained by local purchase. The Directorates concerned have, however, been carefully watching the situation, and all the Administrative Services on the Line of Communications have continued to work with smoothness and regularity, in spite of the increased pressure thrown upon them. In this connection I wish to bring to notice the good service which has been rendered by the Staff of the Base Ports.

The work of the Railway Transport Department has been excellently carried out, and I take this opportunity of expressing my appreciation of the valuable service rendered by the French railway authorities generally, and especially by Colonel Ragueneau, late Directeur des Chemins de Fer, Lieutenant-Colonel Le Hénaff, Directeur des Chemins de Fer, Lieutenant-Colonel Dumont, Commissaire Militaire, Chemin de Fer du Nord, and Lieutenant-Colonel Frid, Commissaire Regulateur, Armée Anglaise.

The Army Postal Service has continued to work well, and at the present time a letter posted in London is delivered at General Headquarters or at the Headquarters of the Armies and Army Corps on the following evening, and reaches an addressee in the trenches on the second day after posting. The delivery of parcels has also been accelerated, and is carried out with regularity and despatch.

His Majesty the King of the Belgians visited the British lines on February 8th and inspected some of the units in reserve behind the trenches.

During the last two months I have been much indebted to His Majesty and his gallant Army for valuable assistance and co-operation in various ways.

His Royal Highness the Prince of Wales is the bearer of this despatch. His Royal Highness continues to make most satisfactory progress. During the Battle of Neuve Chapelle he acted on my General Staff as a Liaison Officer. Reports from the General Officers Commanding Corps and Divisions to which he has been attached agree in commending the thoroughness in which he performs any work entrusted to him.

I have myself been very favourably impressed by the quickness with which His Royal Highness has acquired knowledge of the various branches of the service, and the deep interest he has always displayed in the comfort and welfare of the men.

His visits to the troops, both in the field and in hospitals, have been greatly appreciated by all ranks.

His Royal Highness did duty for a time in the trenches with the Battalion to which he belongs.

In connection with the Battle of Neuve Chapelle I desire to bring to Your Lordship's special notice the valuable services of General Sir Douglas Haig, K.C.B., K.C.I.E., K.C.V.O., A.D.C., Commanding the First Army. I am also much indebted to the able and devoted assistance I have received from Lieutenant-General Sir William Robertson, K.C.B., K.C.V.O., D.S.O., Chief of the General Staff, in the direction of all the operations recorded in this despatch.

I have many other names to bring to notice for valuable, gallant and distinguished service during the period under review, and these will form the subject of a separate report at an early date.

I have the honour to be,
Your Lordship's most obedient Servant,
J. D. P. FRENCH, Field-Marshal,
Commanding-in-Chief,
The British Army in the Field.

∞⚉∞

MILITARY DESPATCH
DATED
15th June, 1915

Published in the Supplement to the "London Gazette", No. 29225, of 10th July, 1915.

From the Field-Marshal Commanding-in-Chief, the British Army in France, to the Secretary of State for War, War Office, London, S.W.

General Headquarters, 15th June, 1915.

MY LORD,

I have the honour to report that since the date of my last despatch (5th April, 1915) the Army in France under my command has been heavily engaged opposite both flanks of the line held by the British Forces.

In the North the town and district of Ypres have once more in this campaign been successfully defended against vigorous and sustained attacks made by large forces of the enemy, and supported by a mass of heavy and field artillery, which, not only in number, but also in weight and calibre, is superior to any concentration of guns which has previously assailed that part of the line.

In the South a vigorous offensive has again been taken by troops of the First Army, in the course of which a large area of entrenched and fortified ground has been captured from the enemy, whilst valuable support has been afforded to the attack which our Allies have carried on with such marked success against the enemy's positions to the east of Arras and Lens.

I much regret that during the period under report the fighting has been characterised on the enemy's side by a cynical and barbarous disregard of the well-known usages of civilised war and a flagrant defiance of the Hague Convention.

All the scientific resources of Germany have apparently been brought into play to produce a gas of so virulent and poisonous a nature that any human being brought into contact with it is first paralysed and then meets with a lingering and agonising death.

The enemy has invariably preceded, prepared and supported his attacks by a discharge in stupendous volume of these poisonous gas fumes whenever the wind was favourable.

Such weather conditions have only prevailed to any extent in the neighbourhood of Ypres, and there can be no doubt that the effect of these poisonous fumes materially influenced the operations in that theatre, until experience suggested effective counter-measures, which have since been so perfected as to render them innocuous.

The brain power and thought which has evidently been at work before this unworthy method of making war reached the pitch of efficiency which has been demonstrated in its practice shows that the Germans must have harboured these designs for a long time.

As a soldier I cannot help expressing the deepest regret and some surprise that an Army which hitherto has claimed to be the chief exponent of the chivalry of war should have stooped to employ such devices against brave and gallant foes.

On the night of Saturday, April 17th, a commanding hill which afforded the enemy excellent artillery observation toward the West and North-West was successfully mined and captured. This hill, known as Hill 60, lies opposite the northern extremity of the line held by the 2nd Corps.

The operation was planned and the mining commenced by Major-General Bulfin before the ground was handed over to the troops under Lieutenant-General Sir Charles Fergusson, under whose supervision the operation was carried out.

The mines were successfully fired at 7 p.m. on the 17th instant, and immediately afterwards the hill was attacked and gained, without difficulty, by the 1st Battalion, Royal West Kent Regiment, and the 2nd Battalion, King's Own Scottish Borderers. The attack was well supported by the Divisional Artillery, assisted by French and Belgian batteries.

During the night several of the enemy's counter-attacks were repulsed with heavy loss, and fierce hand-to-hand fighting took place; but on the early morning of the 18th the enemy succeeded in forcing back the troops holding the right of the hill to the reverse slope, where, however, they hung on throughout the day.

On the evening of the 18th these two battalions were relieved by the 2nd Battalion, West Riding Regiment, and the 2nd Battalion, King's Own Yorkshire Light Infantry, who again stormed the hill under cover of heavy artillery fire, and the enemy was driven off at the point of the bayonet. In this operation 53 prisoners were captured, including four officers.

On the 20th and following days many unsuccessful attacks by the enemy were made on Hill 60, which was continuously shelled by heavy artillery.

On May 1st another attempt to recapture Hill 60 was supported by great volumes of asphyxiating gas, which caused nearly all the men along a front of about 400 yards to be immediately struck down by its fumes.

The splendid courage with which the leaders rallied their men and subdued the natural tendency to panic (which is inevitable on such occasions), combined with the prompt intervention of supports, once more drove the enemy back.

A second and more severe "gas" attack, under much more favourable weather conditions, enabled the enemy to recapture this position on May 5th. The enemy owes his success in this last attack entirely to the use of asphyxiating gas. It was only a few days later that the means, which have since proved so effective, of counteracting this method of making war were put into practice. Had it been otherwise, the enemy's attack on May 5th would most certainly have shared the fate of all the many previous attempts he had made.

It was at the commencement of the Second Battle of Ypres on the evening of the 22nd April, referred to earlier in this report, that the enemy first made use of asphyxiating gas.

Some days previously I had complied with General Joffre's request to take over the trenches occupied by the French, and on the evening of the 22nd the troops holding the lines east of Ypres were posted as follows:—

From Steenstraate to the east of Langemarck, as far as the Poeleappelle Road, a French Division.

Thence, in a south-easterly direction toward the Passchendaele–Becelaere Road, the Canadian Division.

Thence a Division took up the line in a southerly direction east of Zonnebeke to a point west of Becelaere, whence another Division continued the line south-east to the northern limit of the Corps on its right.

Of the 5th Corps there were four battalions in Divisional Reserve about Ypres; the Canadian Division had one battalion in Divisional Reserve and the 1st Canadian Brigade in Army Reserve. An Infantry Brigade, which had just been withdrawn after suffering heavy losses on Hill 60, was resting about Vlamertinghe.

Following a heavy bombardment, the enemy attacked the French Division at about 5 p.m., using asphyxiating gases for the first time. Aircraft reported that at about 5 p.m. thick yellow smoke had been seen issuing from the German trenches between Langemarck and Bixschoote. The French reported that two simultaneous attacks had been made east of the Ypres-Staden Railway, in which these asphyxiating gases had been employed.

What follows almost defies description. The effect of these poisonous gases was so virulent as to render the whole of the line held by the French Division mentioned above practically incapable of any action at all. It was at first impossible for anyone to realise what had actually happened. The smoke and fumes hid everything from sight, and hundreds of men were thrown into a comatose or dying condition, and within an hour the whole position had to be abandoned, together with about 50 guns.

I wish particularly to repudiate any idea of attaching the least blame to the French Division for this unfortunate incident.

After all the examples our gallant Allies have shown of dogged and tenacious courage in the many trying situations in which they have been placed throughout the course of this campaign, it is quite superfluous for me to dwell on this aspect of the incident, and I would only express my firm conviction that, if any troops in the world had been able to hold their trenches in the face of such a treacherous and altogether unexpected onslaught, the French Division would have stood firm.

The left flank of the Canadian Division was thus left dangerously exposed to serious attack in flank, and there appeared to be a prospect of their being overwhelmed and of a successful attempt by the Germans to cut off the British troops occupying the salient to the East.

In spite of the danger to which they were exposed the Canadians held their ground with a magnificent display of tenacity and courage; and it is not too much to say that the bearing and conduct of these splendid troops averted a disaster which might have been attended with the most serious consequences.

They were supported with great promptitude by the reserves of the Divisions holding the salient and by a Brigade which had been resting in billets.

Throughout the night the enemy's attacks were repulsed, effective counter-attacks were delivered, and at length touch was gained with the French right, and a new line was formed.

The 2nd London Heavy Battery, which had been attached to the Canadian Division, was posted behind the right of the French Division, and, being involved in their retreat, fell into the enemy's hands. It was recaptured by the Canadians in their counter-attack, but the guns could not be withdrawn before the Canadians were again driven back.

During the night I directed the Cavalry Corps and the Northumbrian Division, which was then in general reserve, to move to the west of Ypres, and placed these troops at the disposal of the General Officer Commanding the Second Army. I also directed other reserve troops from the 3rd Corps and the First Army to be held in readiness to meet eventualities.

In the confusion of the gas and smoke the Germans succeeded in capturing the bridge at Steenstraate and some works south of Lizerne, all of which were in occupation by the French.

The enemy having thus established himself to the west of the Ypres Canal, I was somewhat apprehensive of his succeeding in driving a wedge between the French and Belgian troops at this point. I directed, therefore, that some of the reinforcements sent north should be used to support and assist General Putz, should he find difficulty in preventing any further advance of the Germans west of the canal.

At about 10 o'clock on the morning of the 23rd connection was finally ensured between the left of the Canadian Division and the French right, about eight hundred yards east of the canal; but as this entailed the maintenance by the British troops of a much longer line than that which they had held before the attack commenced on the previous night, there were no reserves available for counter-attack until reinforcements, which were ordered up from the Second Army, were able to deploy to the east of Ypres.

Early on the morning of the 23rd I went to see General Foch, and from him I received a detailed account of what had happened, as reported by General Putz. General Foch informed me that it was his intention to make good the original line and regain the trenches which the French Division had lost. He expressed the desire that I should maintain my present line, assuring me that the original position would be re-established in a few days. General Foch further informed me that he had ordered up large French reinforcements, which were now on their way, and that troops from the North had already arrived to reinforce General Putz.

I fully concurred in the wisdom of the General's wish to re-establish our old line, and agreed to co-operate in the way he desired, stipulating, however, that if the position was not re-established within a limited time I could not allow the British troops to remain in so exposed a situation as that which the action of the previous twenty-four hours had compelled them to occupy.

During the whole of the 23rd the enemy's artillery was very active, and his attacks all along the front were supported by some heavy guns which had been brought down from the coast in the neighbourhood of Ostend.

The loss of the guns on the night of the 22nd prevented this fire from being kept down, and much aggravated the situation. Our positions, however, were well maintained by the vigorous counter-attacks made by the 5th Corps.

During the day I directed two Brigades of the 3rd Corps, and the Lahore Division of the Indian Corps, to be moved up to the Ypres area and placed at the disposal of the Second Army.

In the course of these two or three days many circumstances combined to render the situation east of the Ypres Canal very critical and most difficult to deal with.

The confusion caused by the sudden retirement of the French Division, and the necessity for closing up the gap and checking the enemy's advance at all costs, led to a mixing up of units and a sudden shifting of the areas of command, which was quite unavoidable. Fresh units, as they came up from the South, had to be pushed into the firing line in an area swept by artillery fire which, owing to the capture of the French guns, we were unable to keep down.

All this led to very heavy casualties; and I wish to place on record the deep admiration which I feel for the resource and presence of mind evinced by the leaders actually on the spot.

The parts taken by Major-General Snow and Brigadier-General Hull were reported to me as being particularly marked in this respect.

An instance of this occurred on the afternoon of the 24th when the enemy succeeded in breaking through the line at St. Julien.

Brigadier-General Hull, acting under the orders of Lieutenant-General Alderson, organised a powerful counter-attack with his own Brigade and some of the nearest available units. He was called upon to control, with only his Brigade Staff, parts of battalions from six separate divisions which were quite new to the ground. Although the attack did not succeed in retaking St. Julien, it effectually checked the enemy's further advance.

It was only on the morning of the 25th that the enemy were able to force back the left of the Canadian Division from the point where it had originally joined the French line.

During the night, and the early morning of the 25th, the enemy directed a heavy attack against the Division at Broodseinde crossroads which was supported by a powerful shell fire, but he failed to make any progress.

During the whole of this time the town of Ypres and all the roads to the East and West were uninterruptedly subjected to a violent artillery fire, but in spite of this the supply of both food and ammunition was maintained throughout with order and efficiency.

During the afternoon of the 25th many German prisoners were taken, including some officers. The hand-to-hand fighting was very severe, and the enemy suffered heavy loss.

During the 26th the Lahore Division and a Cavalry Division were pushed up into the fighting line, the former on the right of the French, the latter in support of the 5th Corps.

In the afternoon the Lahore Division, in conjunction with the French right, succeeded in pushing the enemy back some little distance toward the North, but their further advance was stopped owing to the continual employment by the enemy of asphyxiating gas.

On the right of the Lahore Division the Northumberland Infantry Brigade advanced against St. Julien and actually succeeded in entering, and for a time occupying, the southern portion of that village. They were, however, eventually driven back, largely owing to gas, and finally occupied a line a short way to the South. This attack was most successfully and gallantly led by Brigadier-General Riddell, who, I regret to say, was killed during the progress of the operation.

Although no attack was made on the south-eastern side of the salient, the troops operating to the east of Ypres were subjected to heavy artillery fire from this direction which took some of the battalions, which were advancing North to the attack, in reverse.

Some gallant attempts made by the Lahore Division on the 27th, in conjunction with the French, pushed the enemy further North; but they were partially frustrated by the constant fumes of gas to which they were exposed. In spite of this, however, a certain amount of ground was gained.

The French had succeeded in retaking Lizerne, and had made some progress at Steenstraate and Het Sas; but up to the evening of the 28th no further progress had been made toward the recapture of the original line.

I sent instructions therefore, to Sir Herbert Plumer, who was now in charge of the operation, to take preliminary measures for the retirement to the new line which had been fixed upon.

On the morning of the 29th I had another interview with General Foch, who informed me that strong reinforcements were hourly arriving to support General Putz, and urged me to postpone issuing orders for any retirement until the result of his attack, which was timed to commence at daybreak on the 30th, should be known. To this I agreed, and instructed Sir Herbert Plumer accordingly.

No substantial advance having been made by the French, I issued orders to Sir Herbert Plumer at one o'clock on May 1st to commence his withdrawal to the new line.

The retirement was commenced the following night, and the new line was occupied on the morning of May 4th.

I am of opinion that this retirement, carried out deliberately with scarcely any loss, and in the face of an enemy in position, reflects the greatest possible credit on Sir Herbert Plumer and those who so efficiently carried out his orders.

The successful conduct of this operation was the more remarkable from the fact that on the evening of May 2nd, when it was only half completed, the enemy made a heavy attack, with the usual gas accompaniment, on St. Julien and the line to the west of it.

An attack on a line to the east of Fortuin was made at the same time under similar conditions.

In both cases our troops were at first driven from their trenches by gas fumes, but on the arrival of the supporting battalions and two brigades of a Cavalry Division, which were sent up in support from about Potijze, all the lost trenches were regained at night.

On the 3rd May, while the retirement was still going on, another violent attack was directed on the northern face of the salient. This was also driven back with heavy loss to the enemy.

Further attempts of the enemy during the night of the 3rd to advance from the woods west of St. Julien were frustrated entirely by the fire of our artillery.

During the whole of the 4th the enemy heavily shelled the trenches we had evacuated, quite unaware that they were no longer occupied. So soon as the retirement was discovered the Germans commenced to entrench opposite our new line and to advance their guns to new positions. Our artillery, assisted by aeroplanes, caused him considerable loss in carrying out these operations.

Up to the morning of the 8th the enemy made attacks at short intervals, covered by gas, on all parts of the line to the east of Ypres, but was everywhere driven back with heavy loss.

Throughout the whole period since the first break of the line on the night of April 22nd all the troops in this area had been constantly subjected to violent artillery bombardment from a large mass of guns with an unlimited supply of ammunition. It proved impossible whilst under so vastly superior fire of artillery to dig efficient trenches, or to properly reorganise the line, after the confusion and demoralisation caused by the first great gas surprise and the subsequent almost daily gas attacks. Nor was it until after this date (May 8th) that effective preventatives had been devised and provided. In these circumstances a violent bombardment of nearly the whole of the 5th Corps front broke out at 7 a.m. on the morning of the 8th, which gradually concentrated on the front of the Division between north and south of Frezenberg. This fire completely obliterated the trenches and caused enormous losses.

The artillery bombardment was shortly followed by a heavy infantry attack, before which our line had to give way.

I relate what happened in Sir Herbert Plumer's own words:—

"The right of one Brigade was broken about

10.15 a.m.; then its centre, and then part of the left of the Brigade in the next section to the south. The Princess Patricia's Canadian Light Infantry, however, although suffering very heavily, stuck to their fire or support trenches throughout the day. At this time two battalions were moved to General Headquarters 2nd line astride the Menin road to support and cover the left of their Division.

"At 12.25 p.m. the centre of a Brigade further to the left also broke; its right battalion, however, the 1st Suffolks, which had been refused to cover a gap, still held on and were apparently surrounded and over-whelmed. Meanwhile, three more battalions had been moved up to reinforce, two other battalions were moved up in support to General Headquarters line, and an Infantry Brigade came up to the grounds of Vlamertinghe Chateau in Corps Reserve.

"At 11.30 a.m. a small party of Germans attempted to advance against the left of the British line, but were destroyed by the 2nd Essex Regiment.

"A counter-attack was launched at 3.30 p.m. by the 1st York and Lancaster Regiment, 3rd Middlesex Regiment, 2nd East Surrey Regiment, 2nd Royal Dublin Fusiliers and the 1st Royal Warwickshire Regiment. The counter-attack reached Frezenberg, but was eventually driven back and held up on a line running about north and south through Verlorenhoek, despite repeated efforts to advance. The 12th London Regiment on the left succeeded at great cost in reaching the original trench line, and did considerable execution with their machine gun.

"The 7th Argyll and Sutherland Highlanders and the 1st East Lancashire Regiment attacked in a north-easterly direction towards Wieltje, and connected the old trench line with the ground gained by the counter-attack, the line being consolidated during the night.

"During the night orders were received that two Cavalry Divisions would be moved up and placed at the disposal of the 5th Corps, and a Territorial Division would be moved up to be used if required.

"On the 9th the Germans again repeated their bombardment. Very heavy shell fire was concentrated for two hours on the trenches of the 2nd Gloucestershire Regiment and 2nd Cameron Highlanders, followed by an infantry attack which was successfully repulsed. The Germans again bombarded the salient, and a further attack in the afternoon succeeded in occupying 150 yards of trench. The Gloucesters counter-attacked, but suffered heavily, and the attack failed. The salient being very exposed to shell fire from both flanks, as well as in front, it was deemed advisable not to attempt to retake the trench at night, and a retrenchment was therefore dug across it.

"At 3 p.m. the enemy started to shell the whole front of the centre Division, and it was reported that the right Brigade of this Division was being heavily punished, but continued to maintain its line.

"The trenches of the Brigades on the left centre were also heavily shelled during the day and attacked by infantry. Both attacks were repulsed.

"On the 10th instant the trenches on either side of the Menin–Ypres Road were shelled very severely all the morning. The 2nd Cameron Highlanders, 9th Royal Scots, and the 3rd and 4th King's Royal Rifles, however, repulsed an attack made, under cover of gas, with heavy loss. Finally, when the trenches had been practically destroyed and a large number of the garrison buried, the 3rd King's Royal Rifles and 4th Rifle Brigade fell back to the trenches immediately west of Bellewaarde Wood. So heavy had been the shell fire that the proposal to join up the line with a switch through the wood had to be abandoned, the trees broken by the shells forming an impassable entanglement.

"After a comparatively quiet night and morning (10th–11th) the hostile artillery fire was concentrated on the trenches of the 2nd Cameron Highlanders and 1st Argyll and Sutherland Highlanders at a slightly more northern point than on the previous day. The Germans attacked in force and gained a footing in part of the trenches, but were promptly ejected by a supporting company of the 9th Royal Scots. After a second short artillery bombardment the Germans again attacked about 4.15 p.m., but were again repulsed by rifle and machine-gun fire. A third bombardment followed and this time the Germans succeeded in gaining a trench—or rather what was left of it—a local counter-attack failing. However, during the night the enemy were again driven out. The trench by this time being practically non-existent, the garrison found it untenable under the very heavy shell fire the enemy brought to bear upon it, and the trench was evacuated. Twice more did the German snipers creep back into it, and twice more they were ejected. Finally, a retrenchment was made, cutting off the salient which had been contested throughout the day. It was won owing solely to the superior weight and number of the enemy's guns, but both our infantry and our artillery took a very heavy toll of the enemy, and the ground lost has proved of little use to the enemy.

"On the remainder of the front the day passed comparatively quietly, though most parts of the line underwent intermittent shelling by guns of various calibres.

"With the assistance of the Royal Flying Corps the 31st Heavy Battery scored a direct hit on a German gun, and the North Midland Heavy Battery got on to some German howitzers with great success.

"With the exception of another very heavy burst of shell fire against the right Division early in the morning, the 12th passed uneventfully.

"On the night of the 12th–13th the line was re-organised, the centre Division retiring into Army Reserve to rest, and their places being taken in the trenches by the two Cavalry Divisions; the Artillery and Engineers of the centre Division forming with them what was known as the "Cavalry Force" under the command of General De Lisle.

"On the 13th the various reliefs having been completed without incident, the heaviest bombardment yet experienced broke out at 4.30 a.m. and continued with little intermission throughout the day. At about 7.45 a.m. the Cavalry Brigade astride the railway, having suffered very severely, and their trenches having been obliterated, fell back about 800 yards. The north Somerset Yeomanry on the right of the Brigade, although also suffering severely, hung on to their trenches throughout the day, and actually advanced and attacked the enemy with the bayonet. The Brigade on its right also maintained its position; as did also the Cavalry Division, except the left squadron which, when reduced to sixteen men, fell back. The 2nd Essex Regiment, realising the situation, promptly charged and retook the trench, holding it till relieved by the Cavalry. Meanwhile a counter-attack by two Cavalry Brigades was launched at 2.30 p.m., and succeeded, in spite of very heavy shrapnel and rifle fire, in regaining the original line of trenches, turning out the Germans who had entered it, and in some cases pursuing them for some distance. But a very heavy shell fire was again opened on them, and they were again compelled to retire to an irregular line in rear, principally the craters of shell holes. The enemy in their counter-attack suffered very severe losses.

"The fighting in other parts of the line was little less severe. The 1st East Lancashire Regiment were shelled out of their trenches, but their support company and the 2nd Essex Regiment, again acting on their own initiative, won them back. The enemy penetrated into the farm at the north-east corner of the line, but the 1st Rifle Brigade, after a severe struggle, expelled them. The 1st Hampshire Regiment also repelled an attack, and killed every German who got within fifty yards of their trenches. The 5th London Regiment, despite very heavy casualties, maintained their position unfalteringly. At the southern end of-the line the left Brigade was once again heavily shelled, as indeed was the whole front. At the end of a very hard day's fighting our line remained in its former position, with the exception of the short distance lost by one Cavalry Division. Later, the line was pushed forward, and a new line was dug in a less exposed position, slightly in rear of that originally held. The night passed quietly.

"Working parties of from 1,200 to 1,800 men have been found every night by a Territorial Division and other units for work on rear lines of defence, in addition to the work performed by the garrisons in reconstructing the front line trenches which were daily destroyed by shell fire.

"The work performed by the Royal Flying Corps has been invaluable. Apart from the hostile aeroplanes actually destroyed, our airmen have prevented a great deal of aerial reconnaissance by the enemy, and have registered a large number of targets with our artillery.

"There have been many cases of individual gallantry. As instances may be given the following:—

"During one of the heavy attacks made against our infantry gas was seen rolling forward from the enemy's trenches. Private Lynn of the 2nd Lancashire Fusiliers at once rushed to the machine gun without waiting to adjust his respirator. Single-handed he kept his gun in action the whole time the gas was rolling over, actually hoisting it on to the parapet to get a better field of fire. Although nearly suffocated by the gas, he poured a stream of lead into the advancing enemy and checked their attack. He was carried to his dug-out, but, hearing another attack was imminent, he tried to get back to his gun. Twenty-four hours later he died in great agony from the effects of the gas.

"A young subaltern in a cavalry regiment went forward alone one afternoon to reconnoitre. He got into a wood, 1,200 yards in front of our lines, which he found occupied by Germans, and came back with the information that the enemy had evacuated a trench and were digging another—information which proved most valuable to the artillery as well as to his own unit.

"A patrol of two officers and a non-commissioned officer of the 1st Cambridgeshires went out one night to reconnoitre a German trench 350 yards away. Creeping along the parapet of the trench, they heard sounds indicating the presence of six or seven of the enemy. Further on they heard deep snores, apparently proceeding from a dug-out immediately beneath them. Although they knew that the garrison of the trench outnumbered them, they decided to procure an identification. Unfortunately, in pulling out a clasp knife with which to cut off the sleeper's identity disc, one of the officer's revolvers went off. A conversation in agitated whispers broke out in the

German trench, but the patrol kept safely away, the garrison being too startled to fire.

"Despite the very severe shelling to which the troops had been subjected, which obliterated trenches and caused very many casualties, the spirit of all ranks remains excellent. The enemy's losses, particularly on the 10th and 13th, have unquestionably been serious. On the latter day they evacuated trenches (in face of the cavalry counter-attack) in which were afterwards found quantities of equipment and some of their own wounded. The enemy have been seen stripping our dead, and on three occasions men in khaki have been seen advancing."

The fight went on by the exchange of desultory shell and rifle fire, but without any remarkable incident until the morning of May 24th. During this period, however, the French on our left had attained considerable success. On the 15th instant they captured Steenstraate and the trenches in Het Sas, and on the 16th they drove the enemy headlong over the canal, finding two thousand German dead. On the 17th they made a substantial advance on the east side of the canal, and on the 20th they repelled a German counter-attack, making a further advance in the same direction, and taking one hundred prisoners.

On the early morning of the 24th a violent outburst of gas against nearly the whole front was followed by heavy shell fire, and the most determined attack was delivered against our position east of Ypres.

The hour the attack commenced was 2.45 a.m. A large proportion of the men were asleep, and the attack was too sudden to give them time to put on their respirators.

The 2nd Royal Irish and the 9th Argyll and Sutherland Highlanders, overcome by gas fumes, were driven out of a farm held in front of the left Division, and this the enemy proceeded to hold and fortify.

All attempts to retake this farm during the day failed, and during the night of the 24th–25th the General Officer Commanding the Left Division decided to take up a new line which, although slightly in rear of the old one, he considered to be a much better position. This operation was successfully carried out.

Throughout the day the whole line was subjected to one of the most violent artillery attacks which it had ever undergone; and the 5th Corps and the Cavalry Divisions engaged had to fight hard to maintain their positions. On the following day, however, the line was consolidated, joining the right of the French at the same place as before, and passing through Wieltje (which was strongly fortified) in a southerly direction on to Hooge, where the Cavalry have since strongly occupied the chateau, and pushed our line further east.

In pursuance of a promise which I made to the French Commander-in-Chief to support an attack which his troops were making on the 9th May between the right of my line and Arras, I directed Sir Douglas Haig to carry out on that date an attack on the German trenches in the neighbourhood of

Rougebanc (north-west of Fromelles) by the 4th Corps, and between Neuve Chapelle and Givenchy, by the 1st and Indian Corps.

The bombardment of the enemy's positions commenced at 5 a.m.

Half-an-hour later the 8th Division of the 4th Corps captured the first line of German trenches about Rougebanc, and some detachments seized a few localities beyond this line. It was soon found, however, that the position was much stronger than had been anticipated, and that a more extensive artillery preparation was necessary to crush the resistance offered by his numerous fortified posts.

Throughout the 9th and 10th repeated efforts were made to make further progress. Not only was this found to be impossible, but the violence of the enemy's machine-gun fire from his posts on the flanks rendered the captured trenches so difficult to hold that all the units of the 4th Corps had to retire to their original position by the morning of the 10th.

The 1st and Indian Divisions south of Neuve Chapelle met with no greater success, and on the evening of the 10th I sanctioned Sir Douglas Haig's proposal to concentrate all our available resources on the southern point of attack.

The 7th Division was moved round from the 4th Corps area to support this attack, and I directed the General Officer Commanding the First Army to delay it long enough to ensure a powerful and deliberate artillery preparation.

The operations of the 9th and 10th formed part of a general plan of attack which the Allies were conjointly conducting on a line extending from the north of Arras to the south of Armentières; and, although immediate progress was not made during this time by the British forces, their attack assisted in securing the brilliant successes attained by the French forces on their right, not only by holding the enemy in their front but by drawing off a part of the German reinforcements which were coming up to support their forces east of Arras.

It was decided that the attack should be resumed on the night of the 12th instant, but the weather continued very dull and misty, interfering much with artillery observation. Orders were finally issued, therefore, for the action to commence on the night of the 15th instant.

On the 15th May I moved the Canadian Division into the 1st Corps area and placed them at the disposal of Sir Douglas Haig.

The infantry of the Indian Corps and the 2nd Division of the 1st Corps advanced to the attack of the enemy's trenches which extended from Richebourg L'Avoué in a south-westerly direction.

Before daybreak the 2nd Division had succeeded in capturing two lines of the enemy's trenches, but the Indian Corps were unable to make any progress owing to the strength of the enemy's defences in the neighbourhood of Richebourg L'Avoué.

At daybreak the 7th Division, on the right of the 2nd, advanced to the attack, and by 7 a.m. had entrenched themselves on a line running nearly North and South, half-way between their original trenches and La Quinque Rue, having cleared and captured several lines of the enemy's trenches, including a number of fortified posts.

As it was found impossible for the Indian Corps to make any progress in face of the enemy's defences Sir Douglas Haig directed the attack to be suspended at this point and ordered the Indian Corps to form a defensive flank.

The remainder of the day was spent in securing and consolidating positions which had been won, and endeavouring to unite the inner flanks of the 7th and 2nd Divisions, which were separated by trenches and posts strongly held by the enemy.

Various attempts which were made throughout the day to secure this object had not succeeded at nightfall in driving the enemy back.

The German communications leading to the rear of their positions were systematically shelled throughout the night.

About two hundred prisoners were captured on the 16th instant.

Fighting was resumed at daybreak; and by 11 o'clock the 7th Division had made a considerable advance, capturing several more of the enemy's trenches. The task allotted to this Division was to push on in the direction of Rue D'Ouvert, Chateau St. Roch and Canteleux.

The 2nd Division was directed to push on when the situation permitted towards the Rue de Marais and Violaines.

The Indian Division was ordered to extend its front far enough to enable it to keep touch with the left of the 2nd Division when they advanced.

On this day I gave orders for the 51st (Highland) Division to move into the neighbourhood of Estaires to be ready to support the operations of the First Army.

At about noon the enemy was driven out of the trenches and posts which he occupied between the two Divisions, the inner flanks of which were thus enabled to join hands.

By nightfall the 2nd and 7th Divisions had made good progress, the area of the captured ground being considerably extended to the right by the successful operations of the latter.

The state of the weather on the morning of the 18th much hindered an effective artillery bombardment, and further attacks had, consequently, to be postponed.

Infantry attacks were made throughout the line in the course of the afternoon and evening; but, although not very much progress was made, the line was advanced to the La Quinque Rue–Béthune Road before nightfall.

On the 19th May the 7th and 2nd Divisions were drawn out of the line to rest. The 7th Division was relieved by the Canadian Division and the 2nd Division by the 51st (Highland) Division.

Sir Douglas Haig placed the Canadian and 51st Divisions, together with the artillery of the 2nd and 7th Divisions, under the command of Lieutenant-

General Alderson, whom he directed to conduct the operations which had hitherto been carried on by the General Officer Commanding First Corps; and he directed the 7th Division to remain in Army Reserve.

During the night of the 19th–20th a small post of the enemy in front of La Quinque Rue was captured.

During the night of the 20th–21st the Canadian Division brilliantly carried on the excellent progress made by the 7th Division by seizing several of the enemy's trenches and pushing forward their whole line several hundred yards. A number of prisoners and some machine guns were captured.

On the 22nd instant the 51st (Highland) Division was attached to the Indian Corps, and the General Officer Commanding the Indian Corps took charge of the operations at La Quinque Rue, Lieutenant-General Alderson with the Canadians conducting the operations to the north of that place.

On this day the Canadian Division extended their line slightly to the right and repulsed three very severe hostile counter attacks.

On the 24th and 25th May the 47th Division (2nd London Territorials) succeeded in taking some more of the enemy's trenches and making good the ground gained to the east and north.

I had now reason to consider that the battle, which was commenced by the First Army on the 9th May and renewed on the 16th, having attained for the moment the immediate object I had in view, should not be further actively proceeded with; and I gave orders to Sir Douglas Haig to curtail his artillery attack and to strengthen and consolidate the ground he had won.

In the battle of Festubert above described the enemy was driven from a position which was strongly entrenched and fortified, and ground was won on a front of four miles to an average depth of 600 yards.

The enemy is known to have suffered very heavy losses, and in the course of the battle 785 prisoners and 10 machine guns were captured. A number of machine guns were also destroyed by our fire.

During the period under report the Army under my command has taken over trenches occupied by some other French Divisions.

I am much indebted to General d'Urbal, commanding the 10th French Army, for the valuable and efficient support received throughout the battle of Festubert from three groups of French 75 centimetre guns.

In spite of very unfavourable weather conditions, rendering observation most difficult, our own artillery did excellent work throughout the battle.

During the important operations described above, which were carried on by the First and Second Armies, the 3rd Corps was particularly active in making demonstrations with a view to holding the enemy in its front and preventing reinforcements reaching the threatened area.

As an instance of the successful attempts to deceive the enemy in this respect it may be mentioned that on the afternoon of the 24th instant a bombardment of about an hour was carried out by the 6th Division with the object of distracting attention from the Ypres salient.

Considerable damage was done to the enemy's parapets and wire; and that the desired impression was produced on the enemy is evident from the German wireless news on that day, which stated "West of Lille the English attempts to attack were nipped in the bud."

In previous reports I have drawn attention to the enterprise displayed by the troops of the 3rd Corps in conducting night reconnaissances, and to the courage and resource shown by officers' and other patrols in the conduct of these minor operations.

Throughout the period under report this display of activity has been very marked all along the 3rd Corps front, and much valuable information and intelligence have been collected.

I have much pleasure in again expressing my warm appreciation of the admirable manner in which all branches of the Medical Services now in the field, under the direction of Surgeon-General Sir Arthur Sloggett, have met and dealt with the many difficult situations resulting from the operations during the last two months.

The medical units at the front were frequently exposed to the enemy's fire, and many casualties occurred amongst the officers of the regimental Medical Service. At all times the officers, non-commissioned officers and men, and nurses carried out their duties with fearless bravery and great devotion to the welfare of the sick and wounded.

The evacuation of casualties from the front to the Base and to England was expeditiously accomplished by the Administrative Medical Staffs at the front and on the Lines of Communication. All ranks employed in units of evacuation and in Base Hospitals have shown the highest skill and untiring zeal and energy in alleviating the condition of those who passed through their hands.

The whole organisation of the Medical Services reflects the highest credit on all concerned.

I have once more to call your Lordship's attention to the part taken by the Royal Flying Corps in the general progress of the campaign, and I wish particularly to mention the invaluable assistance they rendered in the operations described in this report, under the able direction of Major-General Sir David Henderson.

The Royal Flying Corps is becoming more and more an indispensable factor in combined operations. In co-operation with the artillery, in particular, there has been continuous improvement both in the methods and in the technical material employed. The ingenuity and technical skill displayed by the officers of the Royal Flying Corps, in effecting this improvement, have been most marked.

Since my last despatch there has been a considerable increase both in the number and in the activity of German aeroplanes in our front. During this period there have been more than sixty combats in the air, in which not one British aeroplane has been lost. As these fights take place almost invariably over or behind the German lines, only one hostile aeroplane has been brought down in our territory. Five more, however, have been definitely wrecked behind their own lines, and many have been chased down and forced to land in most unsuitable ground.

In spite of the opposition of hostile aircraft, and the great number of anti-aircraft guns employed by the enemy, air reconnaissance has been carried out with regularity and accuracy.

I desire to bring to your Lordship's notice the assistance given by the French Military Authorities, and in particular by General Hirschauer, Director of the French Aviation Service, and his assistants, Colonel Bottieaux and Colonel Stammler, in the supply of aeronautical material, without which the efficiency of the Royal Flying Corps would have been seriously impaired.

In this despatch I wish again to remark upon the exceptionally good work done throughout this campaign by the Army Service Corps and by the Army Ordnance Department, not only in the field, but also on the Lines of Communication and at the Base Ports.

To foresee and meet the requirements in the matter of Ammunition, Stores, Equipment, Supplies and Transport has entailed on the part of the officers, non-commissioned officers and men of these Services a sustained effort which has never been relaxed since the beginning of the war, and which has been rewarded by the most conspicuous success.

The close co-operation of the Railway Transport Department, whose excellent work, in combination with the French Railway Staff, has ensured the regularity of the maintenance services, has greatly contributed to this success.

The degree of efficiency to which these Services have been brought was well demonstrated in the course of the Second Battle of Ypres.

The roads between Poperinghe and Ypres, over which transport, supply and ammunition columns had to pass, were continually searched by hostile heavy artillery during the day and night; whilst the passage of the canal through the town of Ypres, and along the roads east of that town, could only be effected under most difficult and dangerous conditions as regards hostile shell fire. Yet, throughout the whole five or six weeks during which these conditions prevailed the work was carried on with perfect order and efficiency.

Since the date of my last report some Divisions of the "New" Army have arrived in this country.

I made a close inspection of one Division, formed up on parade, and have at various times seen several units belonging to others.

These Divisions have as yet had very little experience in actual fighting; but, judging from all I have seen, I am of opinion that they ought to prove a valuable addition to any fighting force.

As regards the Infantry, their physique is excellent, whilst their bearing and appearance on parade reflects great credit on the officers and staffs responsible for their training. The units appear to be thoroughly well officered and commanded. The equipment is in good order and efficient.

Several units of artillery have been tested in the firing line behind the trenches, and I hear very good reports of them. Their shooting has been extremely good, and they are quite fit to take their places in the line.

The Pioneer Battalions have created a very favourable impression, the officers being keen and ingenious and the men of good physique and good diggers. The equipment is suitable. The training in field works has been good, but, generally speaking, they require the assistance of Regular Royal Engineers as regards laying out of important works. Man for man in digging the battalions should do practically the same amount of work as an equivalent number of sappers, and in rivetting, entanglement, &c., a great deal more than the ordinary infantry battalions.

During the months of April and May several divisions of the Territorial Force joined the Army under my command. Experience has shown that these troops have now reached a standard of efficiency which enables them to be usefully employed in complete divisional units.

Several divisions have been so employed; some in the trenches, others in the various offensive and defensive operations reported in this despatch.

In whatever kind of work these units have been engaged, they have all borne an active and distinguished part, and have proved themselves thoroughly reliable and efficient.

The opinion I have expressed in former despatches as to the use and value of the Territorial Force has been fully justified by recent events.

The Prime Minister was kind enough to accept an invitation from me to visit the Army in France, and arrived at my Headquarters on the 30th May.

Mr. Asquith made an exhaustive tour of the front, the hospitals and all the administrative arrangements made by the Corps Commanders for the health and comfort of men behind the trenches. It was a great encouragement to all ranks to see the Prime Minister amongst them; and the eloquent words which on several occasions he addressed to the troops had a most powerful and beneficial effect.

As I was desirous that the French Commander-in-Chief should see something of the British troops, I asked General Joffre to be kind enough to inspect a division on parade.

The General accepted my invitation, and on the 27th May he inspected the 7th Division, under the command of Major-General H. de la P. Gough, C.B., which was resting behind the trenches. General Joffre subsequently expressed to me in a letter the pleasure it gave him to see the British troops, and his appreciation of their appearance on parade. He requested me to make this known to all ranks.

The Moderator of the Church of Scotland, the Right Reverend Dr. Wallace Williamson, Dean of the Order of the Thistle, visited the Army in France between the 7th and 17th May, and made a tour of the Scottish regiments with excellent results.

In spite of the constant strain put upon them by the arduous nature of the fighting which they are called upon to carry out daily and almost hourly, the spirit which animates all ranks of the Army in France remains high and confident.

They meet every demand made upon them with the utmost cheerfulness. This splendid spirit is particularly manifested by the men in hospital, even amongst those who are mortally wounded.

The invariable question which comes from lips hardly able to utter a sound is, "How are things going on at the front?"

In conclusion, I desire to bring to Your Lordship's special notice the valuable services rendered by General Sir Douglas Haig in his successful handling of the troops of the First Army throughout the Battle of Festubert, and Lieutenant-General Sir Herbert Plumer for his fine defence of Ypres throughout the arduous and difficult operations during the latter part of April and the month of May.

I have the honour to be,
Your Lordship's most obedient Servant,
J. D. P. FRENCH, Field-Marshal,
Commanding-in-Chief,
The British Army in France.

∞◦◦❊◦◦∞

MILITARY DESPATCH
FROM THE GENERAL COMMANDING,
MEDITERRANEAN EXPEDITIONARY
FORCE
DATED
20th May, 1915

PUBLISHED IN THE SUPPLEMENT TO THE "LONDON
GAZETTE", No. 29217, OF 6TH JULY, 1915.

From the General Commanding the Mediterranean
Expeditionary Force to the Secretary of State for War,
War Office, London, S.W.

The Dardanelles

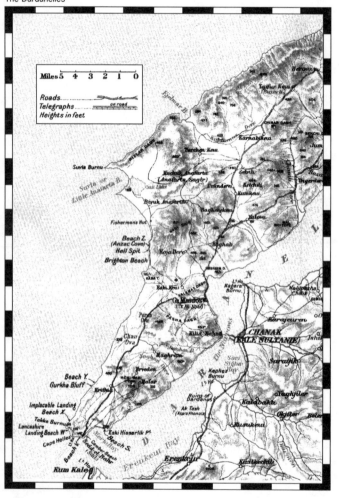

General Headquarters, Mediterranean Expeditionary Force,
20th May, 1915.

MY LORD,

I have the honour to submit my report on the operations in the Gallipoli Peninsula up to and including the 5th May.

In accordance with your Lordship's instructions I left London on 13th March with my General Staff by special train to Marseilles, and thence in H.M.S. "Phæton" to the scene of the naval operations in the Eastern Mediterranean, reaching Tenedos on the 17th March shortly after noon.

Immediately on arrival I conferred with Vice-Admiral de Robeck, Commanding the Eastern Mediterranean Fleet; General d'Amade, Commanding the French Corps Expéditionnaire; and Contre Amiral Guepratte, in command of the French Squadron. At this conference past difficulties were explained to me, and the intention to make a fresh attack on the morrow was announced. The amphibious battle between warships and land fortresses took place next day, the 18th of March. I witnessed these stupendous events, and thereupon cabled your Lordship my reluctant deduction that the co-operation of the whole of the force under my command would be required to enable the Fleet effectively to force the Dardanelles.

By that time I had already carried out a preliminary reconnaissance of the north-western shore of the Gallipoli Peninsula, from its isthmus, where it is spanned by the Bulair fortified lines, to Cape

Helles, at its extremest point. From Bulair this singular feature runs in a south-westerly direction for 52 miles, attaining near its centre a breadth of 12 miles. The northern coast of the northern half of the promontory slopes downwards steeply to the Gulf of Xeros, in a chain of hills, which extend as far as Cape Suvla. The precipitous fall of these hills precludes landing, except at a few narrow gullies, far too restricted for any serious military movements. The southern half of the peninsula is shaped like a badly-worn boot. The ankle lies between Kaba Tepe and Kalkmaz Dagh; beneath the heel lie the cluster of forts at Kilid Bahr, whilst the toe is that promontory, five miles in width, stretching from Tekke Burnu to Sedd-el-Bahr.

The three dominating features in this southern section seemed to me to be:—

(1) Saribair Mountain, running up in a succession of almost perpendicular escarpments to 970 feet. The whole mountain seemed to be a network of ravines and covered with thick jungle.

(2) Kilid Bahr plateau, which rises, a natural fortification artificially fortified, to a height of 700 feet to cover the forts of the Narrows from an attack from the Ægean.

(3) Achi Babi, a hill 600 feet in height, dominating at long field gun range what I have described as being the toe of the peninsula.

A peculiarity to be noted as regards this last southern sector is that from Achi Babi to Cape Helles the ground is hollowed out like a spoon, presenting only its outer edges to direct fire from the sea. The inside of the spoon appears to be open and undulating, but actually it is full of spurs, nullahs and confused under-features.

Generally speaking the coast is precipitous, and good landing-places are few. Just south of Tekke Burnu is a small sandy bay (W), and half a mile north of it is another small break in the cliffs (X). Two miles further up the coast the mouth of a stream indents these same cliffs (Y 2), and yet another mile and a half up a scrub-covered gully looked as if active infantry might be able to scramble up it on to heights not altogether dissimilar to those of Abraham, by Quebec (Y). Inside Sedd-el-Bahr is a sandy beach (V), about 300 yards across, facing a semi-circle of steeply rising ground, as the flat bottom of a half-saucer faces the rim, a rim flanked on one side by an old castle, on the other by a modern fort. By Eski Hissarlik, on the east of Morto Bay (S) was another small beach, which was however dominated by the big guns from Asia. Turning northwards again, there are two good landing places on either side of Kaba Tepe. Farther to the north of that promontory the beach was supposed to be dangerous and difficult. In most of these landing-places the trenches and lines of wire entanglements were plainly visible from on board ship. What seemed to be gun emplacements and infantry redoubts could also be made out through a telescope, but of the full extent of these defences and of the forces available to man them there was no possibility of judging except by practical test.

Altogether the result of this and subsequent reconnaissances was to convince me that nothing but a thorough and systematic scheme for flinging the whole of the troops under my command very rapidly ashore could be expected to meet with success; whereas, on the other hand, a tentative or piecemeal programme was bound to lead to disaster. The landing of an army upon the theatre of operations I have described—a theatre strongly garrisoned throughout, and prepared for any such attempt—involved difficulties for which no precedent was forthcoming in military history except possibly in the sinister legends of Xerxes. The beaches were either so well defended by works and guns, or else so restricted by nature that it did not seem possible, even by two or three simultaneous landings, to pass the troops ashore quickly enough to enable them to maintain themselves against the rapid concentration and counter-attack which the enemy was bound in such case to attempt. It became necessary, therefore, not only to land simultaneously at as many points as possible, but to threaten to land at other points as well. The first of these necessities involved another unavoidable if awkward contingency, the separation by considerable intervals of the force.

The weather was also bound to play a vital part in my landing. Had it been British weather there would have been no alternative but instantly to give up the adventure. To land two or three thousand men, and then to have to break off and leave them exposed for a week to the attacks of 34,000 regular troops, with a hundred guns at their back, was not an eventuality to be lightly envisaged. Whatever happened the weather must always remain an incalculable factor, but at least by delay till the end of April we had a fair chance of several days of consecutive calm.

Before doing anything else I had to redistribute the troops on the transports to suit the order of their disembarkation. The bulk of the forces at my disposal had, perforce, been embarked without its having been possible to pay due attention to the operation upon which I now proposed that they should be launched.

Owing to lack of facilities at Mudros redistribution in that harbour was out of the question. With your Lordship's approval, therefore, I ordered all the transports, except those of the Australian Infantry Brigade and the details encamped at Lemnos Island, to the Egyptian ports. On the 24th March I myself, together with the General Staff, proceeded to Alexandria, where I remained until 7th April, working out the allocation of troops to transports in minutest detail as a prelude to the forthcoming disembarkation. General d'Amade did likewise.

On the 1st April the remainder of the General Headquarters, which had not been mobilised when I left England, arrived at Alexandria.

Apart from the re-arrangements of the troops, my visit to Egypt was not without profit, since it afforded me opportunities of conferring with the G.O.C.

Egypt and of making myself acquainted with the troops, drawn from all parts of the French Republic and of the British Empire, which it was to be my privilege to command.

By the 7th April my preparations were sufficiently advanced to enable me to return with my General Staff to Lemnos, so as to put the finishing touches to my plan in close co-ordination with the Vice-Admiral Commanding the Eastern Mediterranean Fleet.

The covering force of the 29th Division left Mudros Harbour on the evening of 23rd April for the five beaches, S, V, W, X, and Y. Of these, V, W, and X were to be main landings, the landings at S and Y being made mainly to protect the flanks, to disseminate the forces of the enemy, and to interrupt the arrival of his reinforcements. The landings at S and Y were to take place at dawn, whilst it was planned that the first troops for V, W, and X beaches should reach the shore simultaneously at 5.30 a.m. after half an hour's bombardment from the fleet.

The transports conveying the covering force arrived off Tenedos on the morning of the 24th, and during the afternoon the troops were transferred to the warships and fleet-sweepers in which they were to approach the shore. About midnight these ships, each towing a number of cutters and other small boats, silently slipped their cables and, escorted by the 3rd Squadron of the Fleet, steamed slowly towards their final rendezvous at Cape Helles. The rendezvous was reached just before dawn on the 25th. The morning was absolutely still; there was no sign of life on the shore; a thin veil of mist hung motionless over the promontory; the surface of the sea was as smooth as glass. The four battleships and four cruisers which formed the 3rd Squadron at once took up the positions that had been allotted to them, and at 5 a.m., it being then light enough to fire, a violent bombardment of the enemy's defences was begun. Meanwhile the troops were being rapidly transferred to the small boats in which they were to be towed ashore. Not a move on the part of the enemy; except for shells thrown from the Asiatic side of the Straits the guns of the Fleet remained unanswered.

The detachment detailed for S beach (Eski Hissarlik Point) consisted of the 2nd South Wales Borderers (less one company) under Lieut.-Colonel Casson. Their landing was delayed by the current, but by 7.30 a.m. it had been successfully effected at the cost of some 50 casualties, and Lieut.-Col. Casson was able to establish his small force on the high ground near De Totts Battery. Here he maintained himself until the general advance on the 27th brought him into touch with the main body.

The landing on Y beach was entrusted to the King's Own Scottish Borderers and the Plymouth (Marine) Battalion, Royal Naval Division, specially attached to the 29th Division for this task, the whole under the command of Lieut.-Colonel Koe. The beach at this point consisted merely of a narrow strip of sand at the foot of a crumbling scrub-covered cliff some 200 feet high immediately to the west of Krithia.

A number of small gullies running down the face of the cliff facilitated the climb to the summit, and so impracticable had these precipices appeared to the Turks that no steps had been taken to defend them. Very different would it have been had we, as was at one time intended, taken Y 2 for this landing. There a large force of infantry, entrenched up to their necks, and supported by machine and Hotchkiss guns, were awaiting an attempt which could hardly have made good its footing. But at Y both battalions were able in the first instance to establish themselves on the heights, reserves of food, water and ammunition were hauled up to the top of the cliff, and, in accordance with the plan of operations, an endeavour was immediately made to gain touch with the troops landing at X beach. Unfortunately, the enemy's strong detachment from Y 2 interposed, our troops landing at X were fully occupied in attacking the Turks immediately to their front, and the attempt to join hands was not persevered with.

Later in the day a large force of Turks were seen to be advancing upon the cliffs above Y beach from the direction of Krithia, and Colonel Koe was obliged to entrench. From this time onward his small force was subjected to strong and repeated attacks, supported by field artillery, and owing to the configuration of the ground, which here drops inland from the edge of the cliff, the guns of the supporting ships could render him little assistance. Throughout the afternoon and all through the night the Turks made

assault after assault upon the British line. They threw
bombs into the trenches, and, favoured by darkness,
actually led a pony with a machine gun on its back
over the defences and were proceeding to come into
action in the middle of our position when they were
bayonetted. The British repeatedly counter-charged
with the bayonet, and always drove off the enemy for
the moment, but the Turks were in a vast superiority and fresh troops took the place of those who
temporarily fell back. Colonel Koe (since died of
wounds) had become a casualty early in the day, and
the number of officers and men killed and wounded
during the incessant fighting was very heavy. By 7
a.m. on the 26th only about half of the King's Own
Scottish Borderers remained to man the entrench-
ment made for four times their number. These brave
fellows were absolutely worn out with continuous
fighting; it was doubtful if reinforcements could
reach them in time, and orders were issued for
them to be re-imbarked. Thanks to H.M.S.
"Goliath," "Dublin," "Amethyst," and "Sapphire,"
thanks also to the devotion of a small rearguard of
the King's Own Scottish Borderers, which kept off
the enemy from lining the cliff, the re-embarkation
of the whole of the troops, together with the
wounded, stores and ammunition, was safely accomplished, and both battalions were brought round the
southern end of the peninsula. Deplorable as the
heavy losses had been, and unfortunate as was the
tactical failure to make good so much ground at the
outset, yet, taking the operation as it stood, there

can be no doubt it has contributed greatly to the success of the main attack, seeing that the plucky stand made at Y beach had detained heavy columns of the enemy from arriving at the southern end of the peninsula during what it will be seen was a very touch-and-go struggle.

The landing-place known as X beach consists of a strip of sand some 200 yards long by 8 yards wide at the foot of a low cliff. The troops to be landed here were the 1st Royal Fusiliers, who were to be towed ashore from H.M.S. "Implacable" in two parties, half a battalion at a time, together with a beach working party found by the Anson Battalion, Royal Naval Division. About 6 a.m. H.M.S. "Implacable," with a boldness much admired by the Army, stood quite close in to the beach, firing very rapidly with every gun she could bring to bear. Thus seconded, the Royal Fusiliers made good their landing with but little loss. The battalion then advanced to attack the Turkish trenches on the Hill 114, situated between V and W beaches, but were heavily counter-attacked and forced to give ground. Two more battalions of the 87th Brigade soon followed them, and by evening the troops had established themselves in an entrenched position extending from half a mile round the landing-place and as far south as Hill 114. Here they were in touch with the Lancashire Fusiliers, who had landed on W beach. Brigadier-General Marshall, commanding the 87th Brigade, had been wounded during the day's fighting, but continued in command of the brigade.

The landing on V beach was planned to take place on the following lines:—

As soon as the enemy's defences had been heavily bombarded by the fleet, three companies of the Dublin Fusiliers were to be towed ashore. They were to be closely followed by the collier "River Clyde" (Commander Unwin, R.N.), carrying between decks the balance of the Dublin Fusiliers, the Munster Fusiliers, half a battalion of the Hampshire Regiment, the West Riding Field Company, and other details.

The "River Clyde" had been specially prepared for the rapid disembarkation of her complement, and large openings for the exit of the troops had been cut in her sides, giving on to a wide gang-plank by which the men could pass rapidly into lighters which she had in tow. As soon as the first tows had reached land the "River Clyde" was to be run straight ashore. Her lighters were to be placed in position to form a gangway between the ship and the beach, and by this means it was hoped that 2,000 men could be thrown ashore with the utmost rapidity. Further, to assist in covering the landing, a battery of machine guns, protected by sandbags, had been mounted in her bows.

The remainder of the covering force detailed for this beach was then to follow in tows from the attendant battleships.

V beach is situated immediately to the west of Sedd-el-Bahr. Between the bluff on which stands Sedd-el-Bahr village and that which is crowned by No. 1 Fort the ground forms a very regular amphitheatre of three or four hundred yards radius.

The slopes down to the beach are slightly concave, so that the whole area contained within the limits of this natural amphitheatre, whose grassy terraces rise gently to a height of a hundred feet above the shore, can be swept by the fire of a defender. The beach itself is a sandy strip some 10 yards wide and 350 yards long, backed along almost the whole of its length by a low sandy escarpment about 4 feet high, where the ground falls nearly sheer down to the beach. The slight shelter afforded by this escarpment played no small part in the operations of the succeeding thirty-two hours.

At the south-eastern extremity of the beach, between the shore and the village, stands the old fort of Sedd-el-Bahr, a battered ruin with wide breaches in its walls and mounds of fallen masonry within and around it. On the ridge to the north, overlooking the amphitheatre, stands a ruined barrack. Both of these buildings, as well as No. 1 Fort, had been long bombarded by the fleet, and the guns of the forts had been put out of action; but their crumbled walls and the ruined outskirts of the village afforded cover for riflemen, while from the terraced slopes already described the defenders were able to command the open beach, as a stage is overlooked from the balconies of a theatre. On the very margin of the beach a strong barbed-wire entanglement, made of heavier metal and longer barbs than I have ever seen elsewhere, ran right across from the old fort of Sedd-el-Bahr to the foot of the north-western headland. Two-thirds of the way up the ridge a second and even stronger entanglement crossed the amphitheatre, passing in front of the old barrack and ending in the outskirts of the village. A third transverse entanglement, joining these two, ran up the hill near the eastern end of the beach, and almost at right angles to it. Above the upper entanglement the ground was scored with the enemy's trenches, in one of which four pom-poms were emplaced; in others were dummy pom-poms to draw fire, while the débris of the shattered buildings on either flank afforded cover and concealment for a number of machine guns, which brought a cross-fire to bear on the ground already swept by rifle fire from the ridge.

Needless to say, the difficulties in the way of previous reconnaissance had rendered it impossible to obtain detailed information with regard either to the locality or to the enemy's preparations.

As often happens in war, the actual course of events did not quite correspond with the intentions of the Commander. The "River Clyde" came into position off Sedd-el-Bahr in advance of the tows, and, just as the latter reached the shore, Commander Unwin beached his ship also. Whilst the boats and the collier were approaching the landing place the Turks made no sign. Up to the very last moment it appeared as if the landing was to be unopposed. But the moment the first boat touched bottom the storm broke. A tornado of fire swept over the beach, the incoming boats, and the collier. The Dublin Fusiliers and the naval boats' crews suffered exceedingly heavy losses while still in the boats. Those who succeeded in landing and in crossing the strip of sand managed to gain some cover when they reached the low escarpment on the further side. None of the boats, however, were able to get off again, and they and their crews were destroyed upon the beach.

Now came the moment for the "River Clyde" to pour forth her living freight; but grievous delay was caused here by the difficulty of placing the lighters in position between the ship and the shore. A strong current hindered the work and the enemy's fire was so intense that almost every man engaged upon it was immediately shot. Owing, however, to the splendid gallantry of the naval working party, the lighters were eventually placed in position, and then the disembarkation began.

A company of the Munster Fusiliers led the way, but, short as was the distance, few of the men ever reached the farther side of the beach through the hail of bullets which poured down upon them from both flanks and the front. As the second company followed, the extemporised pier of lighters gave way in the current. The end nearest to the shore drifted into deep water, and many men who had escaped being shot were drowned by the weight of their equipment in trying to swim from the lighter to the beach. Undaunted workers were still forthcoming, the lighters were again brought into position, and the third company of the Munster Fusiliers rushed ashore, suffering heaviest loss this time from shrapnel as well as from rifle, pom-pom, and machine-gun fire.

For a space the attempt to land was discontinued. When it was resumed the lighters again drifted into deep water, with Brigadier-General Napier, Captain Costeker, his Brigade Major, and a number of men of the Hampshire Regiment on board. There was nothing for them all but to lie down on the lighters, and it was here that General Napier and Captain Costeker were killed. At this time, between 10 and 11 a.m., about 1,000 men had left the collier, and of these nearly half had been killed or wounded before they could reach the little cover afforded by the steep, sandy bank at the top of the beach. Further attempts to disembark were now given up. Had the troops all been in open boats but few of them would have lived to tell the tale. But, most fortunately, the collier was so constructed as to afford fairly efficient protection to the men who were still on board, and, so long as they made no attempt to land, they suffered comparatively little loss.

Throughout the remainder of the day there was practically no change in the position of affairs. The situation was probably saved by the machine-guns on the "River Clyde," which did valuable service in keeping down the enemy's fire and in preventing any attempt on their part to launch a counter-attack. One half-company of the Dublin Fusiliers, which had been landed at a camber just east of Sedd-el-Bahr village, was unable to work its way across to V beach, and by mid-day had only twenty-five men left. It was proposed to divert to Y beach that part of the main body which had been intended to land on V beach; but this would have involved considerable delay owing to the distance, and the main body was diverted to W beach, where the Lancashire Fusiliers had already affected a landing.

Late in the afternoon part of the Worcestershire Regiment and the Lancashire Fusiliers worked across the high ground from W beach, and seemed likely to relieve the situation by taking the defenders of V beach in flank. The pressure on their own front, however, and the numerous barbed-wire entanglements which intervened, checked this advance, and at nightfall the Turkish garrison still held their ground. Just before dark some small parties of our men made their way along the shore to the outer walls of the Old Fort, and when night had fallen the remainder of the infantry from the collier were landed. A good force was now available for attack, but our troops were at such a cruel disadvantage as to position, and the fire of the enemy was still so accurate in the bright moonlight that all attempts to clear the fort and the outskirts of the village during the night failed one after the other. The wounded who were able to do so without support returned to the collier under cover of darkness; but otherwise the situation at daybreak on the 26th was the same as it had been on the previous day, except that the troops first landed were becoming very exhausted.

Twenty-four hours after the disembarkation began there were ashore on V beach the survivors of the Dublin and Munster Fusiliers and of two companies of the Hampshire Regiment. The Brigadier and his Brigade-Major had been killed; Lieutenant-Colonel Carrington Smith, commanding the Hampshire Regiment, had been killed and the adjutant had been wounded. The Adjutant of the Munster Fusiliers was wounded, and the great majority of the senior officers were either wounded or killed. The remnant of the landing-party still crouched on the beach beneath the shelter of the sandy escarpment which had saved so many lives. With them were two officers of my General Staff—Lieutenant-Colonel Doughty-Wylie and Lieutenant-Colonel Williams. These two officers, who had landed from the "River Clyde," had been striving, with conspicuous contempt for danger, to keep all their comrades in good heart during this day and night of ceaseless imminent peril.

Now that it was daylight once more, Lieutenant-Colonels Doughty-Wylie and Williams set to work to organise an attack on the hill above the beach. Any soldier who has endeavoured to pull scattered units together after they have been dominated for many consecutive hours by close and continuous fire will be able to take the measure of their difficulties. Fortunately, General Hunter Weston had arranged with Rear-Admiral Wemyss about this same time for a heavy bombardment to be opened by the ships upon the Old Fort, Sedd-el-Bahr Village, the Old Castle north of the village, and on the ground leading up from the beach. Under cover of this bombardment, and led by Lieutenant-Colonel Doughty-Wylie and Captain Walford, Brigade-Major R.A., the troops gained a footing in the village by 10 a.m. They encountered a most stubborn opposition and suffered heavy losses from the fire of well-concealed riflemen and machine-guns. Undeterred by the resistance, and supported by the naval gunfire, they pushed forward, and soon after midday they penetrated to the northern edge of the village, whence they were in a position to attack the Old Castle and Hill 141. During this advance Captain Walford was killed. Lieutenant-Colonel Doughty-Wylie had most gallantly led the attack all the way up from the beach through the west side of the village, under galling fire. And now, when, owing so largely to his own inspiring example and intrepid courage, the position had almost been gained, he was killed while leading the last assault. But the attack was pushed forward without wavering, and, fighting their way across the open with great dash, the troops gained the summit and occupied the Old Castle and Hill 141 before 2 p.m.

W beach consists of a strip of deep, powdery sand some 350 yards long and from 15 to 40 yards wide, situated immediately south of Tekke Burnu, where a small gully running down to the sea opens out a break in the cliffs. On either flank of the beach the ground rises precipitously but, in the centre, a number of sand dunes afford a more gradual access to the ridge overlooking the sea. Much time and ingenuity had been employed by the Turks in turning this landing place into a death trap. Close to the water's edge a broad wire entanglement extended the whole length of the shore, and a supplementary barbed network lay concealed under the surface of the sea in the shallows. Land mines and sea mines had been laid. The high ground overlooking the beach was strongly fortified with trenches to which the gully afforded a natural covered approach. A number of machineguns also were cunningly tucked away into holes in the cliff so as to be immune from a naval bombardment whilst they were converging their fire on the wire entanglements. The crest of the hill overlooking the beach was in its turn commanded by high ground to the north-west and south-east, and especially by two strong infantry redoubts near point 138. Both these redoubts were protected by wire entanglements about 20 feet broad, and could be approached only by a bare glacis-like slope leading up from the high ground above W beach or from the Cape Helles lighthouse. In addition, another separate entanglement ran down from these two redoubts to the edge of the cliff near the lighthouse, making intercommunication between V and W beaches impossible until these redoubts had been captured.

So strong, in fact, were the defences of W beach that the Turks may well have considered them impregnable, and it is my firm conviction that no finer feat of arms has ever been achieved by the British soldier—or any other soldier—than the storming of these trenches from open boats on the morning of 25th April.

The landing at W had been entrusted to the 1st Battalion Lancashire Fusiliers (Major Bishop) and it was to the complete lack of the senses of danger or of fear of this daring battalion that we owed our astonishing success. As in the case of the landing at X, the disembarkation had been delayed for half an hour, but at 6 a.m. the whole battalion approached the shore together, towed by eight picket boats in line abreast, each picket boat pulling four ship's cutters. As soon as shallow water was reached, the tows were cast off and the boats were at once rowed to the shore. Three companies headed for the beach and a company on the left of the line made for a small ledge of rock immediately under the cliff at Tekke Burnu. Brigadier-General Hare, commanding the 88th Brigade, accompanied this latter party, which escaped the cross fire brought to bear upon the beach, and was also in a better position than the rest of the battalion to turn the wire entanglements.

While the troops were approaching the shore no shot had been fired from the enemy's trenches, but as soon as the first boat touched the ground a hurricane of lead swept over the battalion. Gallantly led by their officers, the Fusiliers literally hurled themselves ashore and, fired at from right, left and centre, commenced hacking their way through the wire. A long line of men was at once mown down as by a scythe, but the remainder were not to be denied. Covered by the fire of the warships, which had now closed right in to the shore and helped by the flanking fire of the company on the extreme left, they broke through the entanglements and collected under the cliffs on either side of the beach. Here the companies were rapidly reformed, and set forth to storm the enemy's entrenchments wherever they could find them.

In making these attacks the bulk of the battalion moved up towards Hill 114 whilst a small party worked down towards the trenches on the Cape Helles side of the landing-place.

Several land mines were exploded by the Turks during the advance, but the determination of the troops was in no way affected. By 10 a.m. three lines of hostile trenches were in our hands, and our hold on the beach was assured.

About 9.30 a.m. more infantry had begun to disembark, and two hours later a junction was effected on Hill 114 with the troops who had landed on X beach.

On the right, owing to the strength of the redoubt on Hill 138, little progress could be made. The small party of Lancashire Fusiliers which had advanced in this direction succeeded in reaching the edge of the wire entanglements, but were not strong enough to do more, and it was here that Major Frankland, Brigade Major of the 86th Infantry Brigade, who had gone forward to make a personal reconnaissance, was unfortunately killed. Brigadier-General Hare had been wounded earlier in the day, and Colonel Woolly-Dod, General Staff 29th Division, was now sent ashore to take command at W beach and organise a further advance.

At 2 p.m., after the ground near Hill 138 had been subjected to a heavy bombardment, the Worcester Regiment advanced to the assault. Several men of this battalion rushed forward with great spirit to cut passages through the entanglement; some were killed, others persevered, and by 4 p.m. the hill and redoubt were captured.

An attempt was now made to join hands with the troops on V beach, who could make no headway at all against the dominating defences of the enemy. To help them out the 86th Brigade pushed forward in an easterly direction along the cliff. There is a limit, however, to the storming of barbed-wire entanglements. More of these barred the way. Again the heroic wire-cutters came out. Through glasses they could be seen quietly snipping away under a hellish fire as if they were pruning a vineyard. Again some of them fell. The fire pouring out of No. 1 fort grew hotter and hotter, until the troops, now thoroughly exhausted by a sleepless night and by the long day's fighting under a hot sun, had to rest on their laurels for a while.

When night fell, the British position in front of W beach extended from just east of Cape Helles lighthouse, through Hill 138, to Hill 114. Practically every man had to be thrown into the trenches to hold this line, and the only available reserves on this part of our front were the 2nd London Field Company R.E. and a platoon of the Anson Battalion, which had been landed as a beach working party.

During the night several strong and determined counter-attacks were made, all successfully repulsed without loss of ground. Meanwhile the disembarkation of the remainder of the division was proceeding on W and X beaches.

The Australian and New Zealand Army Corps sailed out of Mudros Bay on the afternoon of April

24th, escorted by the 2nd Squadron of the Fleet, under Rear-Admiral Thursby. The rendezvous was reached just after half-past one in the morning of the 25th, and there the 1,500 men who had been placed on board H.M. ships before leaving Mudros were transferred to their boats. This operation was carried out with remarkable expedition, and in absolute silence. Simultaneously the remaining 2,500 men of the covering force were transferred from their transports to six destroyers. At 2.30 a.m. H.M. ships, together with the tows and the destroyers, proceeded to within some four miles of the coast, H.M.S. "Queen" (flying Rear-Admiral Thursby's flag) directing on a point about a mile north of Kaba Tepe. At 3.30 a.m. orders to go ahead and land were given to the tows, and at 4.10 a.m. the destroyers were ordered to follow.

All these arrangements worked without a hitch, and were carried out in complete orderliness and silence. No breath of wind ruffled the surface of the sea, and every condition was favourable save for the moon, which, sinking behind the ships, may have silhouetted them against its orb, betraying them thus to watchers on the shore.

A rugged and difficult part of the coast had been selected for the landing, so difficult and rugged that I considered the Turks were not at all likely to anticipate such a descent. Indeed, owing to the tows having failed to maintain their exact direction the actual point of disembarkation was rather more than a mile north of that which I had selected, and was more closely overhung by steeper cliffs. Although this accident increased the initial difficulty of driving the enemy off the heights inland, it has since proved itself to have been a blessing in disguise, inasmuch as the actual base of the force of occupation has been much better defiladed from shell fire.

The beach on which the landing was actually effected is a very narrow strip of sand, about 1,000 yards in length, bounded on the north and the south by two small promontories. At its southern extremity a deep ravine, with exceedingly steep, scrub-clad sides, runs inland in a north-easterly direction. Near the northern end of the beach a small but steep gully runs up into the hills at right angles to the shore. Between the ravine and the gully the whole of the beach is backed by the seaward face of the spur which forms the north-western side of the ravine. From the top of the spur the ground falls almost sheer, except near the southern limit of the beach, where gentler slopes give access to the mouth of the ravine behind. Further inland lie in a tangled knot the under features of Saribair, separated by deep ravines, which take a most confusing diversity of direction. Sharp spurs, covered with dense scrub, and falling away in many places in precipitous sandy cliffs, radiate from the principal mass of the mountain, from which they run north-west, west, south-west, and south to the coast.

The boats approached the land in the silence and the darkness, and they were close to the shore before the enemy stirred. Then about one battalion of Turks was seen running along the beach to intercept the

lines of boats. At this so critical a moment the conduct of all ranks was most praiseworthy. Not a word
was spoken—everyone remained perfectly orderly
and quiet awaiting the enemy's fire, which sure
enough opened, causing many casualties. The
moment the boats touched land the Australians' turn
had come. Like lightning they leapt ashore, and each
man as he did so went straight as his bayonet at the
enemy. So vigorous was the onslaught that the Turks
made no attempt to withstand it and fled from ridge
to ridge pursued by the Australian infantry.

This attack was carried out by the 3rd Australian
Brigade, under Major (temporary Colonel) Sinclair
Maclagan, D.S.O. The 1st and 2nd Brigades followed
promptly, and were all disembarked by 2 p.m., by
which time 12,000 men and two batteries of Indian
Mountain Artillery had been landed. The disembarkation of further artillery was delayed owing to
the fact that the enemy's heavy guns opened on the
anchorage and forced the transports, which had been
subjected to continuous shelling from his field guns,
to stand further out to sea.

The broken ground, the thick scrub, the necessity
for sending any formed detachments post haste as
they landed to the critical point of the moment, the
headlong valour of scattered groups of the men who
had pressed far further into the peninsula than had
been intended—all these led to confusion and mixing
up of units. Eventually the mixed crowd of fighting
men, some advancing from the beach, others falling
back before the oncoming Turkish supports, solidified

into a semi-circular position with its right about a mile north of Kaba Tepe and its left on the high ground over Fisherman's Hut. During this period parties of the 9th and 10th Battalions charged and put out of action three of the enemy's Krupp guns. During this period also the disembarkation of the Australian Division was being followed by that of the New Zealand and Australian Division (two brigades only).

From 11 a.m. to 3 p.m. the enemy, now reinforced to a strength of 20,000 men, attacked the whole line, making a specially strong effort against the 3rd Brigade and the left of the 2nd Brigade. This counter-attack was, however, handsomely repulsed with the help of the guns of H.M. ships. Between 5 and 6.30 p.m. a third most determined counter-attack was made against the 3rd Brigade, who held their ground with more than equivalent stubbornness. During the night again the Turks made constant attacks, and the 8th Battalion repelled a bayonet charge; but in spite of all the line held firm. The troops had had practically no rest on the night of the 24/25th; they had been fighting hard all day over most difficult country, and they had been subjected to heavy shrapnel fire in the open. Their casualties had been deplorably heavy. But, despite their losses and in spite of their fatigue, the morning of the 26th found them still in good heart and as full of fight as ever.

It is a consolation to know that the Turks suffered still more seriously. Several times our machine guns got on to them in close formation, and the whole surrounding country is still strewn with their dead of this date.

The reorganisation of units and formations was impossible during the 26th and 27th owing to persistent attacks. An advance was impossible until a reorganisation could be effected, and it only remained to entrench the position gained and to perfect the arrangements for bringing up ammunition, water, and supplies to the ridges—in itself a most difficult undertaking. Four battalions of the Royal Naval Division were sent up to reinforce the Army Corps on the 28th and 29th April.

On the night of May 2nd a bold effort was made to seize a commanding knoll in front of the centre of the line. The enemy's enfilading machine guns were too scientifically posted, and 800 men were lost without advantage beyond the infliction of a corresponding loss to the enemy. On May 4th an attempt to seize Kaba Tepe was also unsuccessful, the barbed-wire here being something beyond belief. But a number of minor operations have been carried out, such as the taking of a Turkish observing station; the strengthening of entrenchments; the reorganisation of units; and the perfecting of communication with the landing place. Also a constant strain has been placed upon some of the best troops of the enemy who, to the number of 24,000, are constantly kept fighting and being killed and wounded freely, as the Turkish sniper is no match for the Kangaroo shooter, even at his own game.

The assistance of the Royal Navy, here as elsewhere, has been invaluable. The whole of the arrangements have been in Admiral Thursby's hands, and I trust I may be permitted to say what a trusty and powerful friend he has proved himself to be to the Australian and New Zealand Army Corps.

Concurrently with the British landings a regiment of the French Corps was successfully disembarked at Kum Kale under the guns of the French fleet, and remained ashore till the morning of the 26th, when they were re-embarked. 500 prisoners were captured by the French on this day.

This operation drew the fire of the Asiatic guns from Morto Bay and V beach on to Kum Kale, and contributed largely to the success of the British landings.

On the evening of the 26th the main disembarkation of the French Corps was begun, V beach being allotted to our Allies for this purpose, and it was arranged that the French should hold the portion of the front between the telegraph wire and the sea.

The following day I ordered a general advance to a line stretching from Hill 236 near Eski Hissarlik Point to the mouth of the stream two miles north of Tekke Burnu. This advance, which was commenced at midday, was completed without opposition, and the troops at once consolidated their new line. The forward movement relieved the growing congestion on the beaches, and by giving us possession of several new wells afforded a temporary solution to the water problem, which had hitherto been causing me much anxiety.

By the evening of the 27th the Allied forces had established themselves on a line some three miles long, which stretched from the mouth of the nullah, 3,200 yards north-east of Tekke Burnu, to Eski Hissarlik Point, the three brigades of the 29th Division less two battalions on the left and in the centre, with four French battalions on the right, and beyond them again the South Wales Borderers on the extreme right.

Owing to casualties this line was somewhat thinly held. Still, it was so vital to make what headway we could before the enemy recovered himself and received fresh reinforcements that it was decided to push on as quickly as possible. Orders were therefore issued for a general advance to commence at 8 a.m. next day.

The 29th Division were to march on Krithia, with their left brigade leading, the French were directed to extend their left in conformity with the British movements and to retain their right on the coast-line south of the Kereves Dere.

The advance commenced at 8 a.m. on the 28th, and was carried out with commendable vigour, despite the fact that from the moment of landing the troops had been unable to obtain any proper rest.

The 87th Brigade, with which had been incorporated the Drake Battalion, Royal Naval Division, in the place of the King's Own Scottish Borderers and South Wales Borderers, pushed on rapidly, and by 10 a.m. had advanced some two miles. Here the further progress of the Border regiment was barred by a strong work on the left flank. They halted to concentrate and make dispositions to attack it, and at that moment had to withstand a determined counter-attack by the Turks. Aided by heavy gun fire from H.M.S. "Queen Elizabeth," they succeeded in beating off the attack, but they made no further progress that day, and when night fell entrenched themselves on the ground they had gained in the morning.

The Inniskilling Fusiliers, who advanced with their right on the Krithia ravine, reached a point about three-quarters of a mile south-west of Krithia. This was, however, the farthest limit attained, and later on in the day they fell back into line with other corps.

The 88th Brigade on the right of the 87th progressed steadily until about 11.30 a.m., when the stubbornness of the opposition, coupled with a dearth of ammunition, brought their advance to a standstill. The 86th Brigade, under Lieutenant-Colonel Casson, which had been held in reserve, were thereupon ordered to push forward through the 88th Brigade in the direction of Krithia.

The movement commenced at about 1 p.m., but though small reconnoitring parties got to within a few hundred yards of Krithia, the main body of the brigade did not get beyond the line held by the 88th Brigade. Meanwhile, the French had also pushed on in the face of strong opposition along the spurs on the western bank of the Kereves Dere, and had got to within a mile of Krithia with their right thrown back and their left in touch with the 88th Brigade. Here they were unable to make further progress; gradually the strength of the resistance made itself felt, and our Allies were forced during the afternoon to give ground.

By 2 p.m. the whole of the troops with the exception of the Drake Battalion had been absorbed into the firing line. The men were exhausted, and the few guns landed at the time were unable to afford them adequate artillery support. The small amount of transport available did not suffice to maintain the supply of munitions, and cartridges were running short despite all efforts to push them up from the landing-places.

Hopes of getting a footing on Achi Babi had now perforce to be abandoned—at least for this occasion. The best that could be expected was that we should be able to maintain what we had won, and when at 3 p.m. the Turks made a determined counter-attack with the bayonet against the centre and right of our line, even this seemed exceedingly doubtful. Actually a partial retirement did take place. The French were also forced back, and at 6 p.m. orders were issued for our troops to entrench themselves as best they could in the positions they then held, with their right flank thrown back so as to maintain connection with our Allies. In this retirement the right flank of the 88th Brigade was temporarily uncovered, and the Worcester Regiment suffered severely.

Had it been possible to push in reinforcements in men, artillery and munitions during the day, Krithia should have fallen, and much subsequent fighting for its capture would have been avoided.

Two days later this would have been feasible, but I had to reckon with the certainty that the enemy would, in that same time, have received proportionately greater support. I was faced by the usual choice of evils, and although the result was not what I had hoped, I have no reason to believe that hesitation and delay would better have answered my purpose.

For, after all, we had pushed forward quite appreciably on the whole. The line eventually held by our troops on the night of the 28th ran from a point on the coast three miles north-west of Tekke Burnu to a point one mile north of Eski Hissarlik, whence it was continued by the French south-east to the coast.

Much inevitable mixing of units of the 86th and 88th Brigades had occurred during the day's fighting, and there was a dangerous re-entrant in the line at the junction of the 87th and 88th Brigades near the Krithia nullah. The French had lost heavily, especially in officers, and required time to re-organise.

The 29th April was consequently spent in straightening the line, and in consolidating and strengthening the positions gained. There was a certain amount of artillery and musketry fire, but nothing serious.

Similarly, on the 30th, no advance was made, nor was any attack delivered by the enemy. The landing of the bulk of the artillery was completed and a readjustment of the line took place, the portion held by the French being somewhat increased.

Two more battalions of the Royal Naval Division had been disembarked, and these, together with three battalions of the 88th Brigade withdrawn from the line, were formed into a reserve.

This reserve was increased on the 1st May by the addition of the 29th Indian Infantry Brigade, which released the three battalions of the 88th Brigade to return to the trenches. The Corps Expéditionnaire d'Orient had disembarked the whole of their infantry and all but two of their batteries by the same evening.

At 10 p.m. the Turks opened a hot shell fire upon our position, and half an hour later, just before the rise of the moon, they delivered a series of desperate attacks. Their formation was in three solid lines, the men in the front rank being deprived of ammunition to make them rely only upon the bayonet. The officers were served out with coloured Bengal lights to fire from their pistols, red indicating to the Turkish guns that they were to lengthen their range; white that our front trenches had been stormed; green that our main position had been carried. The Turkish attack was to crawl on hand and knees until the time came for the final rush to be made. An eloquent hortative was signed Von Zowenstern and addressed to the Turkish rank and file who were called upon, by one mighty effort, to fling us all back into the sea.

"Attack the enemy with the bayonet and utterly destroy him!

"We shall not retire one step; for, if we do, our religion, our country and our nation will perish!

"Soldiers! The world is looking at you! Your only hope of salvation is to bring this battle to a successful issue or gloriously to give up your life in the attempt!"

The first momentum of this ponderous onslaught fell upon the right of the 86th Brigade, an unlucky spot, seeing all the officers thereabouts had already been killed or wounded. So when the Turks came right on without firing and charged into the trenches with the bayonet they made an ugly gap in the line. This gap was instantly filled by the 5th Royal Scots (Territorials), who faced to their flank and executed a brilliant bayonet charge against the enemy, and by the Essex Regiment detached for the purpose by the Officer Commanding 88th Brigade. The rest of the British line held its own with comparative ease, and it was not found necessary to employ any portion of the reserve. The storm next broke in fullest violence against the French left, which was held by the Senegalese. Behind them were two British-Field Artillery Brigades and a Howitzer Battery. After several charges and counter-charges the Senegalese began to give ground and a company of the Worcester Regiment and some gunners were sent forward to hold the gap. Later, a second company of the Worcester Regiment was also sent up, and the position was then maintained for the remainder of the night, although, about 2 a.m., it was found necessary to despatch one battalion Royal Naval Division to strengthen the extreme right of the French.

About 5 a.m. a counter-offensive was ordered, and the whole line began to advance. By 7.30 a.m. the British left had gained some 500 yards, and the centre had pushed the enemy back and inflicted heavy losses. The right also had gained some ground in conjunction with the French left, but the remainder of the French line was unable to progress. As the British centre and left were now subjected to heavy cross fire from concealed machine guns, it was found impossible to maintain the ground gained, and therefore, about 11 a.m., the whole line withdrew to its former trenches.

The net result of the operations was the repulse of the Turks and the infliction upon them of very heavy losses. At first we had them fairly on the run, and had it not been for those inventions of the devil—machine guns and barbed wire—which suit the Turkish character and tactics to perfection, we should not have stopped short of the crest of Achi Babi. As it was, all brigades reported great numbers of dead Turks in front of their lines, and 350 prisoners were left in our hands.

On the 2nd, during the day, the enemy remained quiet, burying his dead under a red crescent flag, a work with which we did not interfere. Shortly after 9 p.m., however, they made another attack against the whole allied line, their chief effort being made against the French front, where the ground favoured their approach. The attack was repulsed with loss.

During the night 3rd/4th the French front was again subjected to a heavy attack, which they were able to repulse without assistance from my general reserve.

The day of the 4th was spent in reorganisation, and a portion of the line held by the French, who had lost heavily during the previous night's fighting, was taken over by the 2nd Naval Brigade. The night passed quietly.

During the 5th the Lancashire Fusilier Brigade of the East Lancashire Division was disembarked and placed in reserve behind the British left.

Orders were issued for an advance to be carried out next day, and these and the three days' battle which ensued, will be dealt with in my next despatch.

The losses, exclusive of the French, during the period covered by this despatch were, I regret to say, very severe, numbering:—

177 Officers and 1,990 other ranks killed,
412 Officers and 7,807 other ranks wounded,
13 Officers and 3,580 other ranks missing.

From a technical point of view it is interesting to note that my Administrative Staff had not reached Mudros by the time when the landings were finally arranged. All the highly elaborate work involved by these landings was put through by my General Staff working in collaboration with Commodore Roger Kayes, C.B., M.V.O., and the Naval Transport Officers allotted for the purpose by Vice-Admiral de Robeck. Navy and Army carried out these combined duties with that perfect harmony which was indeed absolutely essential to success.

Throughout the events I have chronicled the Royal Navy has been father and mother to the Army. Not one of us but realises how much he owes to

Vice-Admiral de Robeck; to the warships, French and British; to the destroyers, mine sweepers, picket boats, and to all their dauntless crews, who took no thought of themselves, but risked everything to give their soldier comrades a fair run in at the enemy.

Throughout these preparations and operations Monsieur le Général d'Amade has given me the benefit of his wide experiences of war, and has afforded me, always, the most loyal and energetic support. The landing of Kum Kale planned by me as a mere diversion to distract the attention of the enemy was transformed by the Commander of the Corps Expéditionnaire de l'Orient into a brilliant operation, which secured some substantial results. During the fighting which followed the landing of the French Division at Sedd-el-Bahr no troops could have acquitted themselves more creditably under very trying circumstances, and under very heavy losses, than those working under the orders of Monsieur le Général d'Amade.

Lieutenant-General Sir W. R. Birdwood, K.C.S.I., C.B., C.I.E., D.S.O., was in command of the detached landing of the Australian and New Zealand Army Corps above Kaba Tepe, as well as during the subsequent fighting. The fact of his having been responsible for the execution of these difficult and hazardous operations—operations which were crowned with a very remarkable success—speaks, I think, for itself.

Major-General A. G. Hunter-Weston, C.B., D.S.O., was tried very highly, not only during the landings, but more especially in the day and night attacks and counter attacks which ensued. Untiring, resourceful and ever more cheerful as the outlook (on occasion) grew darker, he possesses, in my opinion, very special qualifications as a Commander of troops in the field.

Major-General W. P. Braithwaite, C.B., is the best Chief of the General Staff it has ever been my fortune to encounter in war. I will not pile epithets upon him. I can say no more than what I have said, and I can certainly say no less.

I have many other names to bring to notice for the period under review, and these will form the subject of a separate report at an early date.

I have the honour to be,
Your Lordship's most obedient Servant,
IAN HAMILTON,
General Commanding Mediterranean Expeditionary Force.

∘∘⧟∘∘

NAVAL DESPATCHES
LANDING OF THE ARMY ON
THE GALLIPOLI PENINSULA
25th–26th April, 1915

PUBLISHED IN THE SUPPLEMENT TO THE "LONDON
GAZETTE", NO. 29264, OF 16TH AUGUST, 1915.

Admiralty, 16th August, 1915.

The following despatch has been received from Vice-Admiral John M. de Robeck, reporting the landing of the Army on the Gallipoli Peninsula, 25th–26th April, 1915.

"Triad," July 1, 1915.

SIR,

I HAVE the honour to forward herewith an account of the operations carried out on the 25th and 26th April, 1915, during which period the Mediterranean Expeditionary Force was landed and firmly established in the Gallipoli peninsula.

The landing commenced at 4.20 a.m. on 25th. The general scheme was as follows:—

Two main landings were to take place, the first at a point just north of Gaba Tepe, the second on the southern end of the peninsula. In addition, a landing was to be made at Kum Kale, and a demonstration in force to be carried out in the Gulf of Xeros near Bulair.

The night of the 24th–25th was calm and very clear, with a brilliant moon, which set at 3 a.m.

The first landing, north of Gaba Tepe, was carried out under the orders of Rear-Admiral C. F. Thursby, C.M.G. His squadron consisted of the following ships:—

Battleships:—Queen, London, Prince of Wales, Triumph, Majestic.
Cruiser:—Bacchante.
Destroyers:—Beagle, Bulldog, Foxhound, Scourge, Colne, Usk, Chelmer, Ribble.
Seaplane Carrier:—Ark Royal.
Balloon Ship:—Manica.
Trawlers:—15.

To "Queen," "London," and "Prince of Wales" was delegated the duty of actually landing the troops.

To "Triumph," "Majestic," and "Bacchante" the duty of covering the landing by gunfire.

In this landing a surprise was attempted. The first troops to be landed were embarked in the battleships "Queen," "London," and "Prince of Wales."

The squadron then approached the land at 2.58 a.m. at a speed of 5 knots. When within a short distance of the beach selected for landing the boats were sent ahead. At 4.20 a.m. the boats reached the beach and a landing was effected.

The remainder of the infantry of the covering force were embarked at 10 p.m., 24th.

The troops were landed in two trips, the operation occupying about half an hour, this in spite of the fact that the landing was vigorously opposed, the surprise being only partially effected.

The disembarkation of the main body was at once proceeded with. The operations were somewhat delayed owing to the transports having to remain a considerable distance from the shore in order to avoid the howitzer and field guns' fire brought to bear on them and also the fire from warships stationed in the Narrows, Chanak.

The beach here was very narrow and continuously under shell fire. The difficulties of disembarkation were accentuated by the necessity of evacuating the wounded; both operations proceeded simultaneously. The service was one which called for great determination and coolness under fire, and the success achieved indicates the spirit animating all concerned. In this respect I would specially mention the extraordinary gallantry and dash shown by the 3rd Australian Infantry Brigade (Colonel E. G. Sinclair Maclagan, D.S.O.), who formed the covering force. Many individual acts of devotion to duty were performed by the personnel of the Navy; these are dealt with below. Here I should like to place on record the good service performed by the vessels employed in landing the second part of the covering force; the seamanship displayed and the rapidity with which so large a force was thrown on the beach is deserving of the highest praise.

On the 26th the landing of troops, guns and stores continued throughout the day; this was a most trying service, as the enemy kept up an incessant shrapnel fire, and it was extremely difficult to locate the well-concealed guns of the enemy. Occasional bursts of fire from the ships in the Narrows delayed operations somewhat but these bursts of fire did not last long, and the fire from our ships always drove the enemy's ships away.

The enemy heavily counter-attacked, and though supported by a very heavy shrapnel fire he could make no impression on our line, which was every minute becoming stronger. By nightfall on the 26th April our position north of Gaba Tepe was secure.

The landing at the southern extremity of the Gallipoli peninsula was carried out under the orders of Rear-Admiral R. E. Wemyss, C.M.G., M.V.O., his squadron consisting of the following ships:—

Battleships:—Swiftsure, Implacable, Cornwallis, Albion, Vengeance, Lord Nelson, Prince George.

Cruisers:—Euryalus, Talbot, Minerva, Dublin.
Fleet Sweepers:—6. Trawlers:—14.

Landings in this area were to be attempted at five different places; the conditions at each landing varied considerably. The position of beaches is given below.

Position of Beach.—"Y" beach, a point about 7,000 yards north-east of Cape Tekeh. "X" beach, 1,000 yards north-east of Cape Tekeh. "W" beach, Cape Tekeh–Cape Helles. "V" beach, Cape Helles–Seddul Bahr. Camber, Seddul Bahr. "S" beach, Eski-Hissarlik Point.

Taking these landings in the above order:—

Landing at "Y" Beach.—The troops to be first landed, the King's Own Scottish Borderers, embarked on the 24th in the "Amethyst" and "Sapphire" and proceeded with the transports "Southland" and "Braemar Castle" to a position off Cape Tekeh. At 4.0 a.m. the boats proceeded to "Y" beach, timing their arrival there at 5.0 a.m., and pulled ashore covered by fire from H.M.S. "Goliath." The landing was most successfully and expeditiously carried out, the troops gaining the top of the high cliffs overlooking this beach without being opposed; this result I consider due to the rapidity with which the disembarkation was carried out and the well-placed covering fire from ships.

The Scottish Borderers were landed in two trips, followed at once by the Plymouth Battalion Royal Marines. These troops met with severe opposition on the top of the cliffs, where fire from covering ships was of little assistance and, after heavy fighting, were forced to re-embark on the 26th. The re-embarkation was carried out by the following ships: "Goliath," "Talbot," "Dublin," "Sapphire," and "Amethyst." It was most ably conducted by the beach personnel and covered by the fire of the warships, who prevented the enemy reaching the edge of the cliff, except for a few snipers.

Landing at "X" Beach.—The 2nd Battalion Royal Fusiliers (two companies and M.G. Section) embarked in "Implacable" on 24th, which ship proceeded to a position off the landing-place, where the disembarkation of the troops commenced at 4.30 a.m. and was completed at 5.15 a.m.

A heavy fire was opened on the cliffs on both sides. The "Implacable" approached the beach, and the troops were ordered to land, fire being continued until the boats were close into the beach. The troops on board the "Implacable" were all landed by 7 a.m. without any casualties. The nature of the beach was very favourable for the covering fire from ships, but the manner in which this landing was carried out might well serve as a model.

Landing at "W" Beach.—The 1st Battalion Lancashire Fusiliers embarked in "Euryalus" and "Implacable" on the 24th, who proceeded to positions off the landing-place, where the troops embarked in the boats at about 4 a.m. Shortly after 5 a.m. "Euryalus" approached "W" beach and "Implacable" "X" beach. At 5 a.m. the covering ships opened a heavy fire on the beach, which was continued up to the last moment before landing. Unfortunately this fire did not have the effect on the extensive wire entanglements and trenches that had been hoped for, and the troops, on landing at 6 a.m., were met with a very heavy fire from rifles, machine guns, and pom-poms, and found the obstructions on the beach undamaged. The formation of this beach lends itself admirably to the defence, the landing-place being commanded by sloping cliffs offering ideal positions for trenches and giving a perfect field of fire. The only weakness in the enemy's position was on the flanks, where it was just possible to land on the rocks and thus enfilade the more important defences. This landing on the rocks was effected with great skill, and some maxims, cleverly concealed in the cliffs and which completely enfiladed the main beach, were rushed with the bayonet. This assisted to a great extent in the success of the landing, the troops, though losing very heavily, were not to be denied and the beach and the approaches to it were soon in our possession.

The importance of this success cannot be overestimated; "W" and "V" beaches were the only two of any size in this area, on which troops, other than infantry, could be disembarked, and failure to capture this one might have had serious consequences as the landing at "V" was held up. The beach was being continuously sniped, and a fierce infantry battle was carried on round it throughout the entire day and the following night. It is impossible to exalt too highly the service rendered by the 1st Battalion Lancashire

Fusiliers in the storming of the beach; the dash and gallantry displayed were superb. Not one whit behind in devotion to duty was the work of the beach personnel, who worked untiringly throughout the day and night, landing troops and stores under continual sniping. The losses due to rifle and machine-gun fire sustained by the boats' crews, to which they had not the satisfaction of being able to reply, bear testimony to the arduous nature of the service.

During the night of the 25th–26th enemy attacked continuously, and it was not till 1 p.m. on the 26th, when "V" beach was captured, that our position might be said to be secure.

The work of landing troops, guns, and stores continued throughout this period and the conduct of all concerned left nothing to be desired.

Landing at "V" Beach.—This beach, it was anticipated, would be the most difficult to capture; it possessed all the advantages for defence which "W" beach had, and in addition the flanks were strongly guarded by the old castle and village of Seddul Bahr on the east and perpendicular cliffs on the west; the whole foreshore was covered with barbed wire entanglements which extended in places under the sea. The position formed a natural amphitheatre with the beach as stage.

The first landing here, as at all other places, was made in boats, but the experiment was tried of landing the remainder of the covering force by means of a collier, the "River Clyde". This steamer had been specially prepared for the occasion under the directions of Commander Edward Unwin; large ports had been cut in her sides and gangways built whereby the troops could reach the lighters which were to form a bridge on to the beach.

"V" beach was subjected to a heavy bombardment similarly to "W" beach, with the same result, *i.e.*, when the first trip attempted to land they were met with a murderous fire from rifle, pom-pom and machine gun, which was not opened till the boats had cast off from the steamboats.

A landing on the flanks here was impossible and practically all the first trip were either killed or wounded, a few managing to find some slight shelter under a bank on the beach; in several boats all were either killed or wounded; one boat entirely disappeared, and in another there were only two survivors. Immediately after the boats had reached the beach the "River Clyde" was run ashore under a heavy fire rather towards the eastern end of the beach, where she could form a convenient breakwater during future landing of stores, &c.

As the "River Clyde" grounded, the lighters which were to form the bridge to the shore were run out ahead of the collier, but unfortunately they failed to reach their proper stations and a gap was left between two lighters over which it was impossible for men to cross; some attempted to land by jumping from the lighter which was in position into the sea and wading ashore; this method proved too costly, the lighter being soon heaped with dead and the disembarkation was ordered to cease.

The troops in the "River Clyde" were protected from rifle and machine-gun fire and were in comparative safety.

Commander Unwin, seeing how things were going, left the "River Clyde" and, standing up to his waist in water under a very heavy fire, got the lighters into position; he was assisted in this work by Midshipman G. L. Drewry, R.N.R., of H.M.S. "Hussar"; Midshipman W. St. A. Malleson, R.N., of H.M.S. "Cornwallis"; Able Seaman W. C. Williams, O.N. 186774 (R.F.R.B. 3766), and Seaman R.N.R. George McKenzie Samson, O.N. 2408A, both of H.M.S. "Hussar."

The bridge to the shore, though now passable, could not be used by the troops, anyone appearing on it being instantly shot down, and the men in "River Clyde" remained in her till nightfall.

At 9.50 a.m. "Albion" sent in launch and pinnace manned by volunteer crews to assist in completing bridge, which did not quite reach beach; these boats, however; could not be got into position until dark owing to heavy fire.

It had already been decided not to continue to disembark on "V" Beach, and all other troops intended for this beach were diverted to "W."

The position remained unchanged on "V" beach throughout the day, men of war and the maxims mounted in "River Clyde" doing their utmost to keep down the fire directed on the men under partial shelter on the beach.

During this period many heroic deeds were performed in rescuing wounded men in the water.

During the night of the 25th–26th the troops in "River Clyde" were able to disembark under cover of darkness and obtain some shelter on the beach and in the village of Seddul Bahr, for possession of which now commenced a most stubborn fight.

The fight continued, supported ably by gunfire from H.M.S. "Albion," until 1.24 p.m., when our troops had gained a position from which they assaulted hill 141, which dominated the situation. "Albion" then ceased fire, and the hill, with the old fort on top, was most gallantly stormed by the troops, led by Lieutenant-Colonel C. H. H. Doughty-Wylie, General Staff, who fell as the position was won. The taking of this hill effectively cleared the enemy from the neighbourhood of the "V" Beach, which could now be used for the disembarkation of the allied armies. The capture of this beach called for a display of the utmost gallantry and perseverance from the officers and men of both services—that they successfully accomplished their task bordered on the miraculous.

Landing on the Camber, Seddul Bahr.—One half company Royal Dublin Fusiliers landed here, without opposition, the Camber being "dead ground". The advance from the Camber, however, was only possible on a narrow front, and after several attempts to enter the village of Seddul Bahr this half company had to withdraw after suffering heavy losses.

Landing at "De Totts" "S" Beach.—The 2nd South Wales Borderers (less one company) and a detachment 2nd London Field Company R.E. were landed

in boats, convoyed by "Cornwallis," and covered by
that ship and "Lord Nelson."

Little opposition was encountered, and the hill
was soon in the possession of the South Wales
Borderers. The enemy attacked this position on the
evening of the 25th and during the 26th, but our
troops were firmly established, and with the assistance
of the covering ships all attacks were easily beaten off.

Landing at Kum Kale.—The landing here was
undertaken by the French.

It was most important to prevent the enemy occupying positions in this neighbourhood, whence he
could bring gun fire to bear on the transports off Cape
Helles. It was hoped that by holding this position it
would be possible to deal effectively with the enemy's
guns on the Asiatic shore immediately east of Kum
Kale, which could fire into Seddul Bahr and De Totts.

The French, after a heavy preliminary bombardment, commenced to land at about 10 a.m., and by
the afternoon the whole of their force had been
landed at Kum Kale. When they attempted to advance
to Yeni Shehr, their immediate objective, they were
met by heavy fire from well-concealed trenches, and
were held up just south of Kum Kale village.

During the night of the 25th–26th the enemy
made several counter-attacks, all of which were easily
driven off; during one of these 400 Turks were captured, their retreat being cut off by the fire from the
battleships.

On the 26th, when it became apparent that no
advance was possible without entailing severe losses

and the landing of large reinforcements, the order was given for the French to withdraw and re-embark, which operation was carried out without serious opposition.

I now propose to make the following more general remarks on the conduct of the operations:—

From the very first the co-operation between army and navy was most happy; difficulties which arose were quickly surmounted, and nothing could have exceeded the tactfulness and forethought of Sir Ian Hamilton and his staff.

The loyal support which I received from Contre-Amiral E. P. A. Guepratte simplified the task of landing the Allied armies simultaneously.

The Russian fleet was represented by H.I.R.M.S. "Askold," which ship was attached to the French squadron. Contre-Amiral Guepratte bears testimony to the value of the support he received from Captain Ivanoff, especially during the landing and reembarkation of the French troops at Kum Kale.

The detailed organisation of the landing could not be commenced until the Army Headquarters returned from Egypt on the 10th April. The work to be done was very great, and the naval personnel and material available small.

Immediately on the arrival of the Army Staff at Mudros, committees, composed of officers of both services, commenced to work out the details of the landing operations, and it was due to these officers' indefatigable efforts that the expedition was ready to land on the 22nd April. The keenness displayed by the

officers and men resulted in a good standard of efficiency, especially in the case of the Australian and
New Zealand Corps, who appear to be natural boat-
men.

Such actions as the storming of the Seddul Bahr
position by the 29th Division must live in history for
ever; innumerable deeds of heroism and daring were
performed; the gallantry and absolute contempt for
death displayed alone made the operations possible.

At Gaba Tepe the landing and the dash of the
Australian Brigade for the cliffs was magnificent—
nothing could stop such men. The Australian and
New Zealand Army Corps in this, their first battle, set
a standard as high as that of any army in history, and
one of which their countrymen have every reason to
be proud.

In closing this despatch I beg to bring to their
Lordships' notice the names of certain officers and
men who have performed meritorious service. The
great traditions of His Majesty's Navy were well
maintained, and the list of names submitted of necessity lacks those of many officers and men who
performed gallant deeds unobserved and therefore
unnoted. This standard was high, and if I specially
mention one particular action it is that of
Commander Unwin and the two young officers and
two seamen who assisted him in the work of establishing communication between "River Clyde" and
the beach. Rear-Admirals R. E. Wemyss, C.M.G.,
M.V.O., C. F. Thursby, C.M.G., and Stuart Nicholson,
M.V.O., have rendered invaluable service. Through-

out they have been indefatigable in their efforts to further the success of the operations, and their loyal support has much lightened my duties and responsibilities.

I have at all times received the most loyal support from the Commanding Officers of His Majesty's ships during an operation which called for the display of great initiative and seamanship.

Captain R. F. Phillimore, C.B., M.V.O., A.D.C., as principal Beach Master, and Captain D. L. Dent, as principal Naval Transport Officer, performed most valuable service.

Other titles in the series

John Profumo and Christine Keeler, 1963

"The story must start with Stephen Ward, aged fifty. The son of a clergyman, by profession he was an osteopath ... his skill was very considerable and he included among his patients many well-known people ... Yet at the same time he was utterly immoral."

The Backdrop
The beginning of the '60s saw the publication of 'Lady Chatterley's Lover' and the dawn of sexual and social liberation as traditional morals began to be questioned and in some instances swept away.

The Book
In spite of the recent spate of political falls from grace, the Profumo Affair remains the biggest scandal ever to hit British politics. The Minister of War was found to be having an affair with a call girl who had associations with a Russian naval officer at the height of the Cold War. There are questions of cover-up, lies told to Parliament, bribery and stories sold to the newspapers. Lord Denning's superbly written report into the scandal describes with astonishment and fascinated revulsion the extraordinary sexual behaviour of the ruling classes. Orgies, naked bathing, sado-masochistic gatherings of the great and good and ministers and judges cavorting in masks are all uncovered.

ISBN 0 11 702402 3   Price £6.99

The Loss of the Titanic, 1912

"From 'Mesabe' to 'Titanic' and all east bound ships. Ice report in Latitude 42N to 41.25N; Longitude 49 to 50.30W. Saw much Heavy Pack Ice and a great number of Large Icebergs. Also Field Ice. Weather good. Clear."

The Backdrop

The watchwords were "bigger, better, faster, more luxurious" as builders of ocean-going vessels strove to outdo each other in their race to capitalise on a new golden age of travel.

The Book

The story of the sinking of the *Titanic*, as told by the official enquiry, reveals some remarkable facts which have been lost in popular re-tellings of the story. A ship of the same line, only a few miles away from the *Titanic* as she sank, should have been able to rescue passengers, so why did this not happen? Readers of this fascinating report will discover that many such questions remain unanswered and that the full story of a tragedy which has entered into popular mythology has by no means been told.

ISBN 0 11 702403 1   Price £6.99

Tragedy at Bethnal Green: 1943

"Immediately the alert was sounded a large number of people left their houses in the utmost haste for shelter. A great many were running. Two cinemas at least in the near vicinity disgorged a large number of people and at least three omnibuses set down their passengers outside the shelter."

The Backdrop

The beleaguered East End of London had borne much of the brunt of the Blitz but, in 1943, four years into WWII, it seemed that the worst of the bombing was over.

The Book

The new unfinished tube station at Bethnal Green was one of the largest air raid shelters in London. After a warning siren sounded on 3 March 1943, there was a rush to the shelter. By 8.20pm, a matter of minutes after the alarm had sounded, 174 people lay dead, crushed in their attempt to get into the tube station's booking hall. At the official enquiry, questions were asked about the behaviour of certain officials and whether the accident could have been prevented.

ISBN 0 11 702404 X   Price £6.99

The Judgement of Nuremberg, 1946

"Efficient and enduring intimidation can only be achieved either by Capital Punishment or by measures by which the relatives of the criminal and the population do not know the fate of the criminal. This aim is achieved when the criminal is transferred to Germany."

The Backdrop

WWII is over, there is a climate of jubilation and optimism as the Allies look to rebuilding Europe for the future but the perpetrators of Nazi War crimes have still to be reckoned with, and the full extent of their atrocities is as yet widely unknown.

The Book

Today, we have lived with the full knowledge of the extent of Nazi atrocities for over half a century and yet they still retain their power to shock. Imagine what it was like as they were being revealed in the full extent of their horror for the first time. In this book the judges at the Nuremberg Trials take it in turn to describe the indictments handed down to the defendants and their crimes. The entire history, purpose and method of the Nazi party since its foundation in 1918 is revealed and described in chilling detail.

ISBN 0 11 702406 6   Price £6.99

The Boer War 1900: Ladysmith and Mafeking

"4th February – From General Sir Redvers Buller to Field-Marshal Lord Roberts … I have today received your letter of 26 January. White keeps a stiff upper lip, but some of those under him are desponding. He calculates he has now 7000 effectives. They are eating their horses and have very little else. He expects to be attacked in force this week … "

The Backdrop

The Boer War is often regarded as one of the first truly modern wars, as the British Army, using traditional tactics, came close to being defeated by a Boer force which deployed what was almost a guerrilla strategy in punishing terrain.

The Book

Within weeks of the outbreak of fighting in South Africa, two sections of the British Army were besieged at Ladysmith and Mafeking. Beginning with despatches describing the losses suffered by the British Army at Spion Kop on its way to rescue the garrison at Ladysmith, the book goes on to describe the lifting of the siege. The second part of the book gives Lord Baden Powell's account of the siege of Mafeking and how the soldiers and civilians coped with the inevitable hardship.

ISBN 0 11 702408 2 Price £6.99

The British Invasion of Tibet: Colonel Younghusband, 1904

"On the 13th January I paid ceremonial visit to the Tibetans at Guru, six miles further down the valley in order that by informal discussion I might assure myself of their real attitude. There were present at the interview three monks and one general from Lhasa. These monks were low-bred persons, insolent, rude and intensely hostile; the generals, on the other hand, were polite and well-bred."

The Backdrop

At the turn of the century, the British Empire was at its height, with its army at the forefront of the mission to bring what the Empire saw as the tremendous civilising benefits of the British way of life to those nations which it regarded as still languishing in the dark ages.

The Book

In 1901, a British missionary force under the leadership of Colonel Francis Younghusband crossed over the border from British India and invaded Tibet. Younghusband insisted on the presence of the Dalai Lama at meetings to give tribute to the British and their Empire. The Dalai Lama merely replied that he must withdraw. Unable to tolerate such an insolent attitude, Younghusband marched forward and inflicted considerable defeats on the Tibetans in several one-sided battles.

ISBN 0 11 702409 0   Price £6.99

War 1914: Punishing the Serbs

" ... I said that this would make it easier for others such as Russia to counsel moderation in Belgrade. In fact, the more Austria could keep her demand within reasonable limits, and the stronger the justification she could produce for making any demands, the more chance there would be for smoothing things over. I hated the idea of a war between any of the Great Powers, and that any of them should be dragged into a war by Serbia would be detestable."

The Backdrop

In Europe before WWI, diplomacy between the Embassies was practised with a considered restraint and politeness which provided an ironic contrast to the momentous events transforming Europe forever.

The Book

Dealing with the fortnight leading up to the outbreak of the First World War, the book mirrors recent events in Serbia to an astonishing extent. Some argued for immediate and decisive military action to punish Serbia for the murder of the Archduke Franz Ferdinand. Others pleaded that a war should not be fought over Serbia. The powers involved are by turn angry, conciliatory and, finally, warlike. Events take their course as the great war machine grinds into action.

ISBN 0 11 702410 4   Price £6.99

War 1939: Dealing with Adolf Hitler

"Herr Hitler asserted that 'I did not care how many Germans were being slaughtered in Poland'. This gratuitous impugnment of the humanity of His Majesty's Government and of myself provoked a heated retort on my part and the remainder of the interview was of a somewhat strong character."

The Backdrop

As he presided over the rebuilding of a Germany shattered and humiliated after WWI, opinion regarding Hitler and his intentions was divided and the question of whether his ultimate aim was military domination by no means certain.

The Book

Sir Nevile Henderson, the British ambassador in Berlin in 1939, describes here, in his report to Parliament, the failure of his mission and the events leading up to the outbreak of war. He tells of his attempts to deal with both Hitler and von Ribbentrop to maintain peace and gives an account of the changes in German foreign policy regarding Poland.

ISBN 0 11 702411 2   Price £6.99

The Strange Story of Adolph Beck

"He said he was Lord Winton de Willoughby. He asked why I lived alone in a flat. I said I had an income and wished to do so … Two or three hours after he had gone I missed some tigers' claws and the teeth of an animal mounted in silver with my monogram."

The Backdrop

The foggy streets of Edwardian London were alive with cads, swindlers, ladies of dubious reputation and all manner of low life who fed on human frailty.

The Book

In 1895, Adolph Beck was arrested and convicted of the crimes of deception and larceny. Using the alias Lord Winton de Willoughby, he had entered into the apartments of several ladies, some of whom preferred, for obvious reasons, not to give their names. The ladies gave evidence, as did a handwriting expert, and Mr Beck was imprisoned. But an utterly bizarre sequence of events culminated in a judge who declared that, since he could himself determine perfectly whether the accused was of the criminal classes or not, juries should never be allowed to decide the outcome of a trial. The account given here is of one of the strangest true stories in the entire British legal history.

ISBN 0 11 702414 7   Price £6.99